HAROLD A. T. BENNETT'S
selection from

FATHER ANDREW'S MEDITATIONS FOR EVERY DAY

MOWBRAY
LONDON & OXFORD

PREFACE

THE 180 meditations in this selection comprise just about half the material in Father Andrew's original volume *Meditations for Every Day*, which went to its eleventh impression in 1963.

Unlike the earlier volume, this present book is not linked to the Church Calendar and Lectionary, but may be used daily or dipped into at particular times for spiritual sustenance. Each meditation is complete in itself.

Father Andrew was one of three priests who in 1894 founded the Society of Divine Compassion in the East End of London. Until his death in 1946 he attracted a wide following of people who looked to him as their spiritual guide and counsellor. Many of his writings are of lasting value and this selection of his meditations is here without textual change.

H.A.T.B.

INTRODUCTION

Reprinted from the original edition

S. TERESA, in one of her self-revealings, says that there was a time in her spiritual experience when she always wanted to have a book with her when she went to her prayer, even though she might not open it ; and, just as it gives the preacher confidence sometimes to have his notes with him in the pulpit, although he may not refer to them, there is a time in the spiritual lives of most of us when it is a distinct help to have a book as a companion when we come to our prayer. It is humbly hoped that this book may serve that purpose. In the matter of spiritual reading it is always much more important to spend a certain time in reading than to read a certain number of books ; the books matter very little in comparison with the time spent. As in art the painter's palette always tends to become more simple, so in the life of prayer the need of books becomes less ; but, for all that, even as one should never wholly lay aside vocal prayer, so one should never wholly lay aside the help that books can give one in times of prayer.

The meditations that follow have all had their origin in the time of prayer. Every one of them came into being either in a chapel or in a religious cell before the crucifix. No one of them was written at a study table. So that the author can at any rate say this, that he is sharing with his readers his own meditations. He sincerely hopes that, as they have helped him, they will also help them to look out through the lattices of this life towards the wide liberties through which at last the soul shall soar to God.

ANDREW, s.d.c.

Feast of S. James, 1934

CONTENTS

CONTENTS

CONTENTS

CONTENTS

THE IDEAL AND THE RULE

'He that walketh in a perfect way, he shall serve Me.'—Ps. ci. 6

IDEALS are one thing, rules of life another. Ideals belong to the land of our dreams and desires, rules of life to the level of a common day. Ideals soar heavenwards, rules walk the pavement. Ideals point to the heights to which we hope to rise, rules register the standard beneath which we dare not fall.

It is the Church's business to keep before us the ideal of the perfect life. It is our business to make some rule that shall be as a firm pathway beneath our feet, walking firmly on which we may follow the glory that goes before us. However high we fly, we need firm ground to start from. Let us try to consider of what stuff we should make the substance of our road.

Faith is a firm foundation, feeling is not : faith in God, faith in goodness, faith in good people. Regularity is a firm foundation, fits and starts are not : regular prayer, regular worship, regular meditation, regular self-scrutiny. A religious principle which is the interior soul of one's life is a firm foundation, a little religious colouring which is just an exterior department of one's life is not.

From the ground that our rule of life gives us to stand upon, and with the steadiness of vision that it makes possible for us, we can look upwards to the ideal of a Christian. The ideal of a Christian and a Catholic can be nothing less than this, that he may show forth Christ in his human nature as Christ revealed God in the human nature which He took of the Blessed Virgin Mary. God has seen His end in Christ : our end is found when He sees Christ in us.

THE CLOUD OF GLORY

The Son of Man coming in a cloud with power and great glory.'
S. LUKE xxi. 27

IT is not God's way to create things by magic, to bid them be in a finished form by a word. His way is ever the way of evolution and development. By the same token His revelation of Himself was not by a blaze of glory, which should tell all His secrets at once. God comes to us veiled. The Son of Man cometh in a cloud : so in the ancient Church it was through the visions of prophets that the Messianic idea emerged. So sure was the vision of Isaiah that, had he returned to earth and stood before his Lord on Calvary, he could hardly have painted a truer picture than he did when he spoke of the suffering Servant, 'the man of sorrows, acquainted with grief.'

It was through the cloud of the Incarnation, through the bearing of the Son of Man, that the Son of God revealed Himself to our race, and He is coming to us always through the cloud of His providence, shaping things to fashion His kingdom.

On the Mount of the Transfiguration we are told that the three apostles entered into the cloud and were afraid, but the cloud was not opaque, nor was it silent. There shone through it glory, there appeared in it saints, it was vocal with the voice of the Father. If by the grace of God there may be given to us a mystic sense, we shall see an unfolding purpose in the history of the universe. It is the Son of Man coming in a cloud with power that shall one day be revealed as glory.

MESSENGERS

'My messenger.'—S. MATT. xi. 10

THE first beginnings of life are always messengers of some-thing greater. When God said, ' Let there be light,' the coming of that light was the messenger that something greater was coming. Then life came, and that life was the messenger of increasingly greater life, till there stood on this earth our first parents, and they were messengers of greater life still.

A messenger does not compose his message, he tells it, and that is what is meant by inspiration. The messenger is taught of God. The prophets and the poets of old, looking forward to a greater life that was to be manifested, were none the less messengers of Christ because they did not fully realize how the Christ would come. Then came that wonderful person, John the Baptist, of whom our Lord spoke as ' My messenger,' the last of the Lord's messengers before our Lord Himself came to be the messenger of a kingdom of God and a glory and splendour beyond our dreams.

All of us are missing our vocation in life if we are not messengers of the King, and all our development should be the messenger of a greater development. We are called first to be children of Christ, and that childhood is a message that one day we are to be servants of Christ, and our service is a presage that one day perhaps we may be martyrs for Christ. Our religion should never be a dull thing. We must catch this thrill, this cumulative thought of first the beginning, then the development, and then the fulfilment. We must never be content to remain where we are. We are the messengers of the new age, of the Christ that is to be, messengers of the splendour of the kingdom of God.

PERFECT THROUGH SUFFERINGS

'Perfect through sufferings.'—HEB. ii. 10

THE Old Testament is as full as the New of examples of the way in which the saints of God have been made perfect through suffering. In the first part of the Bible the triumph is largely material, in the New Testament it is spiritual. There was Joseph, who had one trial after another. He was sold by his brethren to the Midianites and became a slave in Egypt; his master's wife treated him shamefully, and he spent a long time in prison for no fault of his own before he was freed. Then he passed swiftly from his prison bondage to the most exalted place in Egypt. But if Joseph sat on the right hand of Pharaoh, S. Stephen saw Jesus at the right hand of God. Joseph knew a material success; Stephen, the first martyr, had a spiritual vision. But both Joseph and Stephen were sustained by the same thing, a deep interior confidence in God.

The holier and greater the saint is, the more interior is the grace which God gives, and the more is the character exalted through sacrifice of some kind, and often through very great suffering. S. Teresa at the end of her life used to say, ' I want to suffer or to die.' She had had in such a real way the experience that when she was in trouble she learnt most about God, that she began to be in love with suffering. A certain Dominican Prioress, Theodosia Drane, gave her Sisters great edification at a time of her life when she wrote in her diary, ' It seemed to me through this time that God was dead.' She had no sensible experience of the presence of God during that time, but what her Sisters saw was a soul becoming a saint.

PEARLS OF GREAT PRICE

'A merchant man . . . when he had found one pearl of great price, went and sold all that he had, and bought it.'

S. MATT. xiii. 45, 46

UNION with God is so great a treasure that it is unthinkable that it could be purchased by any less sum than the total giving of all we have to give. If we are to arrive at God and rest in Him, we shall have to leave all that is not God and find no rest save in Him, and it will only be God Who knows what we leave and what we are sacrificing. We have to be drawn right apart from creatures, if we are intimately to know God. The Cross was to our Lord the consummation of the whole way of His life. The complete darkness and death was the condition of the complete union and glory.

There are two pearls of great price. One is the pearl of human life, and God sold all that He had that He might purchase that. The other is the pearl of perfect union with God, and man has to sell all that he has that he may purchase it. In the great revelation of the Cross we see Man, our Lord in our human nature, selling all that He has and dying naked in the dark that He may purchase the pearl of great price, union with God. We see that achieved, the pearl of great price bought and possessed. Again as we look at Christ upon the Cross, we see God selling all that He has that He may purchase the pearl which is of great price to Him, the soul of His human child. In the cry of the thief upon the Cross, ' Remember me,' and in the winning of the thief's soul, we see the soul of His child, purchased at this awful price, bought and possessed by God.

THE REVELATION OF THE
INCARNATE WORD

'Jesus Christ, the same yesterday, and to-day, and for ever'
HEB. xiii. 8

IT is well constantly to remind ourselves that Bethlehem and Calvary are *revelations*, not *alterations*, of the Divine Being. It is true that in the Incarnation and the Sacred Passion God added to His divine experience a human experience, but there could be no change in the divine character. What is different is our knowledge and consequently our responsibility.

Some of our hymns suggest that the birth at Bethlehem and the death on Calvary are things that God got through and has done with. The children are taught to sing—

> Not in that poor lowly stable,
> With the oxen standing by,
> We shall see Him, but in heaven,
> Set at God's right hand on high.

That may be a true expression of the Divine Transcendence, but if it suggests that, having once descended to Bethlehem, God has since retired to eternal leisure, then it is shaping an altogether distorted vision of God for the child's mind.

Bethlehem *reveals* the everlasting sympathy of God with human needs. Whenever a child is born under those slum conditions which our Lord accepted in order to make them impossible, we do see Him still in the lowly stable. *There* is the Babe of Bethlehem. Calvary *reveals* the divine sorrow for human sorrow, the way in which God is hurt by human sin 'The Cross is the mirror of the love of God and the measure of the sin of man.' Wherever there are executions, wherever men make torture for one another, there, in that darkness, shines out a thorn-crowned Face. It is the Face of God. Calvary is the self-disclosure of what has always been, of what will always be, in the heart of God, as long as the conditions which fashioned the episode of Calvary continue anywhere in God's universe.

CONTRASTS

OUR religion has a double character. It is the revealed religion of God Himself : it is also the crown of natural religion.

The Catholic religion is cosmic. It gathers into itself all the best thought of all the world. God has been working His purposes out in all the great movements of history. Greek thought, Roman order, and the Jewish genius for religion were the immediate preparation for the Gospel ; and by the same token all that is best in modern movements and all that is true in modern science will, we may be sure, be gathered into the treasury of the Church for the ultimate purpose of the glory of God.

On the other hand, the Gospel is a clear-cut thing, which may bring into life something absolutely revolutionary and catastrophic, subversive of all our preconceived ideas. Our Lord said constantly, ' Ye have heard . . but I say . . .' something very different. He not only sowed seed in prepared ground, but also brought a surgeon's knife to cut out that which was diseased. ' If thine eye offend thee, pluck it out.'

We find the same principle in personal religion, which can be both evolutionary and catastrophic. Some lives, like those of S. Paul and S. Francis of Assisi, have the experience of a spiritual storm, through which the soul swiftly passes to the calm of a certain conviction. Other souls evolve without much consciousness of their own evolution, but those about them can see the mellowing of their character, as through their secret prayer they react to the revelation of the Light of the World. Though there is a strong contrast between catastrophic and evolutionary experience, both equally come from God or may be over-ruled by God, and have their parallel in the story of the evolution of the universe.

7

THE FOUR POINTS OF THE CROSS

'The preaching of the Cross.'—I Cor. i. 18

THE first point of the Cross is *consecration*. Our Lord has consecrated all life, and perhaps most of all suffering and sorrow. The Christian may feel that suffering is the touch of Christ's thorns upon his head, of Christ's Cross upon his shoulder, and sorrow a vigil with Him in Gethsemane.

Our Lord's life was one of deliberate and constant giving, the giving of Himself. With Him in His purity it must always have been a positive act of self-oblation. With us in our sinfulness there will constantly be a negative act of self-denial. We can only give ourselves if we deny ourselves, but it is the lower, unreal self which is denied, and the higher, real self which is expressed. Though it may be a cross to refuse the evil, for the evil is often very attractive, yet the good which we must choose is really much more attractive. Self-renunciation is a splendid joyous thing. As the physical athlete finds joy in the power and ease that his body gains by his exercises, so the spiritual athlete gets joy and freedom by a right mortification. The second point of the Cross is *self-renunciation*.

Then the Cross is the great sign of *love*. Our Lord in love and silence accepted injustice and ingratitude. If we take them in silence and sweetness, and give in return real love, we get a deep and tender and wonderful inner sense of union with Christ.

The fourth point is *courage* Let us accept the cost of a true following of the way of the Cross Our Lord cried, ' Father, if it be possible, let this cup pass from Me.' It is not strange that we should often wince under the pain of a perfect following of Christ.

THE FOUR KINDS OF CROSSES

'Endure hardness, as a good soldier of Jesus Christ.'—2 Tɪᴍ. ii. 3

As there are four points to the Cross, so there are four kinds of crosses. There is, first of all, *the exterior cross*, which is formed of all those natural trials which we must all know, through sickness or bereavement or whatever exterior circumstances come to us. All of us, the good, the bad, the indifferent, have at some time to bear an exterior cross.

Secondly, there is *the interior cross*, which any sensitive soul has to know, consisting of spiritual trials, temptation, interior dryness or darkness, all sorts of interior fears and feelings of spiritual pain.

Thirdly, what may be called *the cross of necessity*, that which our daily duty demands of us in the stewardship of what we hold for our Lord's sake. Nothing that we have, do we have really for ourselves. All Christians are called to live their lives as stewards. They must think of the opportunity of riches or the possession of talents as a stewardship laid upon them by God.

Lastly, there is *the cross of love*, when we feel ourselves called by our own deliberate act to give up some good thing that we might honourably keep, as an act of sacrifice for the kingdom's sake. The mark of the Christian in the world is stewardship : the mark of the religious, who is called out of the world, is holy poverty. In this passage from the stewardship of possession for the love of God to the holy poverty that renounces the loved thing for the love of God, consists the cross of love which some of our Lord's lovers are called to carry,

9

THE CENTURION'S SERVANT

'As thou hast believed, so be it done unto thee.'—S. MATT. viii. 13

THE episode of the healing of the centurion's servant teaches us the universality of our Lord's love. This grace bestowed upon a Gentile is something very precious to the mind of S. Luke, who gives a more detailed account in his Gospel. He tells us that the centurion's servant ' was dear unto him.' The centurion had a naturally Christian heart, for he loved his slave. He was also a man of great faith, and seems to have realized something of the unique nature of our Lord's power. He believed that He had a supernatural authority that would enable Him to heal without being personally present, and his faith did not go without its reward.

In all God's intercourse with us, the promise and its conditions are inseparable. If the conditions are fulfilled, the fulfilment of the promise follows. Of necessity, what God is to us depends on what we are willing to be to Him. In prayer the unlimited promise, 'Ask whatsoever ye will,' has for its condition, 'if ye abide in Me.' It is clear that if our union with Christ is as intimate as the union of the branch with the vine, we shall pray wholly with the mind of Christ and only desire what He in our conditions would have desired, and so shall have His experience in prayer fulfilled in our own lives.

There is something peculiarly gracious in the sentence, ' As thou hast believed, so be it done unto thee.' It is as if a rich man who put a gold coin into a beggar's hand said to him sweetly, ' Your hand has made you rich.' Faith is the hand which takes the gift of God : it is not our faith but God's grace that makes us rich, but His courtesy can call it **our** faith.

THE DIVINE NECESSITY

'He must needs pass through Samaria.'—S. JOHN iv. 4, R.V.

WE have *our* necessities, and—here is a wonderful thought—God has *His* necessities. Our necessity is that of the creature who hungers, who goes wearily seeking for some solution of life's mystery.

We may think of creation as of God yielding to the divine desire to express Himself. The creation of each one of us is the expression of something in the mind of our Creator. Having made us in His own image, He must be true to His own nature and love us to the uttermost. His necessity is the necessity of love manifest in holiness. He must needs go to Bethlehem and to the Cross. He must needs seek the soul of this poor woman of Samaria. According to our standards she was not even respectable, but our Lord thought it worth His while to speak to her, in some of the most wonderful sentences that have ever been uttered on earth, of the purity and depth of the spiritual life. She, like every human being, is really a representative of the race, wanting a faith, a religion, a vocation, and He gives her all these things in Himself.

He must needs come seeking every one of His children. It is the divine necessity of Love to desire that the creatures He has created shall be perfect characters, characters like His own, perfect in purity and love, and, that they may be, He will go to every length that love can go. Each one of us is precious to Him beyond our dreams. S. Bernard says, 'The reason for loving God is God.' S. John says, 'We love Him, because He first loved us.'

THE PRESENCE IN THE STORM

'What manner of man is this ?'—S. MATT. viii. 27

THE result of the experience of the storm to the apostles in the episode told by S. Matthew was that they came to a great conviction about our Lord's Person and of the sufficiency of His Presence in any crisis. They turned their gaze from the storm to Him. They did not say, ' What manner of winds and waves are these that have become so suddenly still ? ' but they said, '.What manner of man is this, that even the winds and the sea obey Him ? '

All through the history of the Church persecution of one kind or another, attacks open or veiled, have made conditions such as might best be symbolized by a ship hardly making headway through opposing storms. Again and again the fabric of the ship must have seemed insufficient to ride out the storm. What spiritual sufficiency could there be in a Church with a Papal army or a State establishment, the tool of a French King or the sport of an English Parliament ? Neither the ship nor the crew suggests confidence, as we trace the chart of the voyage through the ages. The tempest has been tremendous, the ship frail, the crew fearful : how is it that the ship has not foundered, how is it that the crew can have hope ?

The answer is this : there is a Presence in the ship. Whenever any humble seaman, frightened by the storm, finds that Presence, he knows the experience of 'a great calm.' The Presence is the calm, our Lord Jesus Christ is our peace, the haven where we would be. To-day as then, though the tempest may cause dismay and the ship and the crew appear inadequate to the crisis of the storm, those who rest in His Presence shall know ' a great calm.'

THE WAY OF PEACE

'To guide our feet into the way of peace.'—S. LUKE i. 79

THERE are many ways through life—a way of pleasure and a way of pain, a way of perplexity, and in this prophecy of Zacharias a way of peace. What is that way, and how may it be brought about ? The first thing necessary about a way is to know whither it leads. The way that leads to God will be the way of peace.

The way of peace is the way of truth. We are not afraid of truth : what we *are* afraid of is anything less than the truth, a half-truth. We must have our minds at rest about God, and know that this life of ours is the work of a Creator and fashioned to fulfil a design worthy of Him.

Again, the way of peace must often be the way of penitence, as it is always the way of love. If we have stained and troubled consciences, the way of peace will be to us the way to the forgiveness of God, which is the true end to true penitence. When Blessed Mary and S. Joseph lost the Holy Child, they had to go back to where they had lost Him, and we have to do that over and over again in life.

The way of peace is also the way of holiness. It is the way of development of our character. All our experiences, what-ever they are, may be to us occasions of attaining to greater holiness through the grace of God, and thereby an experience of deeper peace.

THE STILL SMALL VOICE

WE read in the story of Elijah on the mountain-side how there came a mighty wind that rent the rocks, but he felt that God was not in the wind. Then there came the terrifying experience of an earthquake, but there was that in him which was altogether unmoved by the earthquake, or the fire that followed. Then there came a still small voice, and when that voice, speaking in the very deep of him, said, ' What doest thou here, Elijah ? ' he knew that he must answer.

The Old Testament tells us of the wind and the earthquake and the fire. Though God manifested Himself *by* those things, He was not *in* them ; but God was in the still small voice of the Babe of Bethlehem. God spoke in the Incarnation, and just as the spiritual development of Elijah enabled him to see that the wind and the earthquake and the fire were comparatively unimportant, but that God was in the still small voice, so old Simeon was able to recognize in the little Babe in His Mother's arms the Incarnate Word of God.

We read of stars that are millions of times bigger than our earth, so that our world is smaller than a grain of sand compared with the immensity of the universe and we ourselves less than the tiniest insect. But all this, like the earthquake and the fire, is as nothing compared with the majesty of the still small voice in the soul of man. When that voice challenges us with the question, ' What doest thou here ?' we know that, at whatever cost or sacrifice, we can only find peace when we are able to say, ' I am here to do Thy will.'

THE OMEGA

'I am . . . Omega . . . the end.'—Rev. xxi. 6

SOMETIMES we think we are never going to get to the end of a thing. We may be climbing in a hilly country, and we think that when we get to *that* hill-top we shall be at the top ; but when we get there we find there is yet another peak beyond, and then another and another. We wonder if we are ever going to get to the end of our climb, but there *is* an end ; and, if it is important that we should get to the end, it is necessary that we should be plucky and persevere. We must keep the end in sight, or at any rate in thought, and go on.

It may be that what we think is the end is not really the end at all. There was an actor who used to end his letters always, ' Yours till the Curtain.' But when the curtain descends, though it is the end of the play, it is really the beginning of the players. The king ceases to be a king, the queen ceases to be a queen, and they all suddenly become what they really are, just tired men and women.

Success is not the end : prosperity is not the end : victory is not the end. The Lord Jesus knew very well that Calvary was not the end ; but He knew that Calvary was the way to the end, and ' for the joy that was before Him ' He endured the Cross. God Himself is the end, but the Incarnation of our Lord has provided us with the way to the end. Through the Spirit we know the Son, and through the Son we know the Father, Whom to know is everlasting life, and in that knowledge is the end of life.

LABOUR

'Let him labour . . . that he may have whereof to give.'
EPH. iv. 28, R.V.

HERE we have a good Christian principle. The motive of labour should not be gain or power in themselves, but rather the gain of power to give. We have to labour that we may give good things to our neighbour   But we shall only learn to do this if we have learnt to lift our labour to a fellowship of co-operation with God. The girl or boy who is working unselfishly to support the home is, though perhaps quite unconsciously, fulfilling this principle.

Science, art, and religion are all quests of absolutes : they seek ends, not means. Science seeks absolute truth, and the reward of the seeker is in the truth that he finds ; art seeks absolute beauty, and the dawn of beauty upon him is the artist's reward ; religion seeks absolute reality, and the purity which is born by pain and prayer wins the pure heart which is able to see the vision of God. Labour which is guided by truth and refined by beauty will surely fashion a contribution to life which shall be a true expression of the religion of the Incarnation.

There is a beautiful little prayer : ' Lord, make us masters of ourselves, in order that we may be servants of others.' We can always remember that there is a labour close at hand, and that the most important of all, the double task of self-effacement and self-donation. There is no greater labour really than the attainment to a complete self-mastery. All the work of the ministry in our Lord's life, and all the splendour of His courage and patience in the last week of His Passion, were without a doubt the fruit of that conquest of self which He had learnt during the years at Nazareth and the days in the wilderness.

LIFE AND LABOUR

'Why stand ye here all the day idle ?'—S. Matt. xx. 6

The parable of the Labourers in the Vineyard gives us a thought by which to fashion our lives, and a light on social conditions. We are all meant to be labourers. God Himself is a labourer. ' My Father worketh and I work,' said our Lord. Labour has sometimes been thought of as a commodity that working-men have a right to sell at the best price they can get. Labour ought to be looked upon as an honourable condition, the condition of every one in this world of ours. In the ideal State every one should be working because he loves his work ; every one should give according to his capacity, and should be paid according to his need.

In our spiritual life we are all meant to be labourers. In our prayer, in our communion, in our intercourse with one another, we must try to put in the very best we can. We must give according to our capacity. The point of the parable does not seem to be that some people came at the eleventh hour and a death-bed repentance is better than nothing, but that people have different capacity. We must all give the best we can give, and we can be perfectly certain we shall receive according to our need.

Our Lord was a labouring man, scarred not only with nails on Mount Calvary but with the rough work of the carpenter's shop. In His prayer, in His temptations, in His comradeship, He gave His absolute best, and was supplied with sufficient power to go through all difficulties and consummate His Sacrifice. There is given to us the vocation to labour, and there is promised to us grace sufficient for our needs.

THE SHARING OF THE BURDEN

'Cast thy burden upon the Lord, and He shall sustain thee.'—Ps. lv. 22

IF we cast our burden upon the Lord, the promise is not that He will take it away, but that He will sustain us. ' He will nourish thee ' is another translation; He will give us strength to bear it.

How are we going to do it ? It is to be in our own personal Christian life, our deliberate communion with God in simple prayer, as we acknowledge our faults and spread before Him our perplexities, and gain in those precious moments of waiting upon His will the sense of vocation to go on and the assurance that we shall not go on alone.

In the Upper Room our Lord gave to His disciples not only the communion of the Last Supper, but the privilege of sharing with Him something of His Passion and His pain. God does give to us that privilege, and we may dare to think that we can give to Him a like privilege, and that even as He asked His apostles to watch with Him one hour and accepted the humble help of dear black Simon of Cyrene in bearing His Cross to Calvary, we may cast upon His sympathetic shoulders the burden of our own pain and ask Him to share with us the carrying of the cross that our vocation in life brings to us. We share our pleasures with our acquaintances, and perhaps with some friends our problems, but it is only to our very greatest friends that we accord the honour of a share in our deepest sorrows, and it is only God Himself that can know the real agony of our repentance and the deep sorrow for our sins.

OTHER PEOPLE'S BURDENS

'Bear ye one another's burdens.'—GAL. vi. 2

WHAT are we here for ? We are here for exactly the same reason that our Lord was in this world. He has revealed in His life what human life is for. It is for the fulfilment of a perfect sonship. Our Lord has revealed to us the Father : we are in our measure to reveal the Christ. Our Lord bore the world's burden, revealing His Father as the ever-lasting Love. We are, in bearing one another's burdens, revealing the everlasting brotherhood in Christ.

As Christ drew all men to Himself because He was the revelation of the love of God, so the Church will draw all men to her, when she really reveals Christ. We know that the Church has had her faults and failures, but for all that she has had her saints, and it is in the ranks of the Church that the greatest beauty of the spiritual life has been made manifest. Every one of us can point to hypocrites and can find hypocrisy in our own lives, but the ideal remains true for all that. We are called to be saints, and we shall best bear one another's burdens as we try to keep our own lives pure and our own prayer real.

The first and best gift we can give to the world in which we live and work is the gift of praying personalities. We must be true to our stewardship, ever seeking to raise and never to lower the standard of our life of prayer. We need to bring our spiritual consciousness to our Lord that we may learn to think as He does. When we reach out hands that are consecrated by wounds, we shall really be able to bear one another's burdens.

THE SOWER

'A sower went out to sow his seed.'—S. LUKE viii. 5

EVERY one of us is a sower. The farmers and workers in the fields are sowers in a very literal sense. A teacher is a sower of such seed as will produce the nation of the future. Fathers and mothers are very definitely sowers. They have created life with the co-operation of God, and the life they have created will depend very much upon their influence. Every one who is working, producing food, building up a town, is in some sense a sower.

Every one is a sower of influence, and that is a more subtle thing. All of us are leaving behind us slowly and surely an influence. We have got wills, and can sow what we will, the good or the bad or the indifferent. We can be the enemy of God, the enemy of good, we can sow the evil thing ; or we can sow the good seed of love and unselfish service.

After all, what a man sows is himself. This is true of author, artist, or politician. Surely he sows himself. It is what he is that is expressed in his word, his art, or his policy. Our Lord spoke a parable about Himself : ' Except a corn of wheat fall into the ground and die, it abideth alone : but if it die, it bringeth forth much fruit.' ' They who follow Christ must be content with sowing.' We ourselves were not sown that we might enjoy the fruit of our own lives, but that, learning to die, of the travail of our dying might be born the fruit that should be food for the feeding of the nation of God.

THE CONSECRATION OF THE COMMONPLACE

'That which cometh upon me daily.'—2 Cor. xi. 28

In the Second Epistle to the Corinthians we get a glimpse of what S. Paul's burdens were. He tells us how he was scourged, stoned, shipwrecked, beset by robbers, all sorts of things that came upon him, and then he speaks of ' that which cometh upon me daily.' Very few people probably will be called to endure those special things which S. Paul had to meet, but all of us have this in common, that we have to glorify God in that which comes upon us daily.

Our life is made up of our relationship to God and our contacts with people and things. Every day brings its succession of silences, conversations, activities, contacts of one kind and another. What we must aim at is the consecration of the commonplace, the realization of the splendour of the ordinary day. Our environment may be a difficult one, and we may have difficult temperaments with which to live, but it is just in those things that we may find the great adventure. If we bring them to our Lord, it will be revealed to us that in these contacts is given to us by the divine appointment the way of our development towards sanctity. God does not like ' reach-me-downs ' : ready-made articles are not to His taste. It is His way to create a being with possibilities, giving to His creature the power of development and by His gifts of grace sharing with His creature in that development.

The scene may appear common and the experience drab, but just as the stark hill of Calvary shines for ever with the dawn above it, because of the Love that was revealed there, so our own ordinary life may have an extraordinary beauty, if by the loving oblation of our will it is really consecrated to the Lord of Calvary.

THE DAILY ROUND

*'In the uprightness of mine heart I have willingly offered
all these things.'*—I Chron. xxix. 17

THERE has often been a wrong sort of dualism in people's
minds. They have thought of here and hereafter, time and
eternity, things secular and things sacred. What we want to
try to get is a unifying principle that can make life really one,
and bring all things into consistency. Time is only part of
eternity : hereafter is really here. We have not to get
somewhere to get to God. He can never be nearer to us
than He is now, because in Him we live and move and have
our being. It is the apprehension of that God Who is with
us now that we want to get.

The art of the spiritual life is to link *all* the different
happenings of our daily life on to the one golden thread of
vocation. S. Paul's care was 'the care of all the Churches.'
Our care may be the care of a family, the care of a business,
but it is just this ordinary daily task which may be for us the
way of splendour and the means of union with our God.
Life need have no rivalries. A sense of vocation links up
all the days and duties of a life. If a row of pearls is strung
upon a thread, as long as the thread passes through those
pearls they are all held together in ordered beauty. But if
the thread breaks, the pearls fall apart, and the order and
beauty are lost. If every act of our day is threaded with
the thought of vocation, all the duties and incidents of life
will become the means by which we glorify God and attain
to the knowledge of His love.

JACOB'S LADDER

'Behold a ladder set up on the earth, and the top of it reached to heaven.'—GEN. xxviii. 12

JACOB's Ladder is the symbol of the Sacred Humanity, and the vision which came to him was the revelation of the nearness of God at all times. ' God was in this place,' he said, ' and I knew it not.' It was not that God *came* there, but that God *was* there. The discovery was of a Presence with him in the wilderness, when he had a stone for his pillow and thought he was far away from home.

As the ladder in the sleeper's vision linked earth to heaven, so the Incarnation of our Lord gives to every human life that will accept God's gift of His dear Son the joy of a realized sonship. We may have a stone for a pillow : the Son of God sometimes had not even that. But ' God is in this place,' and since the feet of Jesus have pressed our earth we know it. We have to learn to know a God Whose humility could stoop to Bethlehem and Whose generosity could go to Calvary. The ladder from heaven to earth meets us where we are. Its lowest rung is in the humility of Bethlehem ; its highest in the Sacrifice of Calvary. By this way we also can climb to the experience which our Lord knew, as He in our nature passed from the way of the wilderness to the wonder of His heavenly victory.

COURAGE

'Be strong and of a good courage.'—JOSHUA i. 6

THERE is a very great deal in life to perplex us and try our faith But if we suppose that life was given to us that it might draw out courage, and has been created by God in order that it might develop itself by His grace into something noble and splendid, we begin to get light on it.

It is a brave thing to be penitent, to get down on our knees and ask for the courage to face our souls and the fact of our own failure. Every saint is a penitent; only the bravery of their penitence went very far, and they had the courage of faith. The virtues of humility and courage shine in their halos. When they fell, they got up again and owned their fault ; they fell again, and again they rose, until the day came when they fell and rose and fell no more, because the courage of their faith had won the victory.

The courage of love is the finest of all. If we would be brave, let us learn to love. The courage of the love of Christ took Him to the Cross to die by the side of Dismas the thief ; it took Him amongst publicans and sinners, to the scandal of the Pharisee of His day. If we really love Jesus, and believe that the great God once walked this earth in human form and was ready to go to the gallows to save a poor man wrecked in the storms of life, there should be born of this faith the threefold courage of penitence, faith, and love, that shall make us brave to follow Him along life's road, even if it leads us to a cross.

ALMSGIVING, PRAYER, AND FASTING

'When ye fast.'—S. Matt. vi. 16

In the sixth chapter of his Gospel S. Matthew records what may have been his own personal memories of our Lord's comparison of the ideals of the kingdom of God with the practice of the professing religious people of His day. The Pharisees considered themselves, and were considered by other people, to be examples of religion, and their practice took form in the three energies of almsgiving, prayer, and fasting.

Our Lord accepts and endorses these three religious activities as the principal acts of the spiritual life. But He teaches a holier motive for each than was as a rule the basis of the religion of the Scribes and Pharisees. With them too often prayer was incantation, almsgiving and fasting self-advertisement, and the reward they sought exterior recognition. Our Lord, as always, lifted what He touched to the sphere of eternity. He showed that almsgiving should really stand for all our relations to others, prayer for all our contacts with God, and that fasting should include all personal self-discipline by which we seek to gain reality in our spiritual lives. In a word, He taught us to seek for reality, and the reward He promised was the attainment to reality.

It is a false spirituality that despises the idea of a reward. It is not the reward, but the character of the reward that is sought, that gives the key to the quality of the action. ' The Father that seeth in secret shall reward you openly ' seems to mean that a true interior life will have a quite manifest effect on those who lead it. The person who really prays will become spiritual, the person who really fasts will become free, the person who really gives will become happy.

PRAYER

Prayer is the outgoing of our personality to seek union with our Lord Jesus Christ, a union which will make our own individuality more real and personal. Personality is unity in variety, the one self, as it finds and expresses itself through outgoings and withholdings, becoming in the school of experience shaped to a certain spiritual form. Prayer is the definite determining of this form to be a likeness to our Lord Jesus Christ, that the soul which is God's child may show the lineaments proper to its high heredity and bear the family likeness of the Elder Brother of the great family of mankind.

As personality is unity in variety, so prayer is variety in unity. The unity is that of the self going always out to seek the friendship of Christ, the variety the many ways through which that friendship is claimed and experienced. If, as the Epistle to the Hebrews teaches us, God has spoken unto us by divers portions and in divers manners, through indirect approach and in ascending degrees of nearness, and then, last of all, in the expression of a Word which was Himself, prayer, which is man's response to the great appeal, the reflex action of the soul answering to the Creator's revelation, will follow a way which is not altogether unlike the divine way. We shall speak to God too in divers manners and by divers degrees, in ascending stages of directions and reality, and, last of all, in the expression of a word which is our very self. Prayer, which begins with asking, thinking, and thanking, becomes at last the spiritual outgoing of the whole personality to God in union with the love and patience and Passion of our Lord Jesus Christ, in act and thought, silences and sufferings, more than in uttered words.

'IF'

'If Thou be the Son of God.'—S. Matt. iv. 3

' I could do such a lot,' people sometimes say, ' if I had the time,' or the money, or the ability. That little word ' if' makes a tremendous challenge. We are either accidents or animals or the children of God. If we are accidents, there is not much point in life, and we can only wait till that other accident which we call death comes to end this accident which we call existence. If we are animals, we can only live as animals and die as animals and fight as animals. But if we really are the children of God, we must be rising ever to the splendour and royalty of the everlasting Divine Life, to the majesty, glory, and beauty worthy of God. We are called to love Him with all our heart and soul and strength, and our brothers and sisters, our neighbours, as ourselves.

Lent brings before us a picture of temptation, of our Lord tempted to act in ways that were inconsistent with being the Son of that God Who is His Father and ours. Temptation went all through our Lord's life, as it goes through the lives of all men. All of us are tempted to doubt that we are the children of God. If we are anything less than that, we shall not be ready to face the cross. But if we *are* His children, then we would surely prefer any pain that came to us through doing His will rather than effect an escape, if by escaping we lost our union with Him. It may be that the way of faith will take us through darkness and pain, but if we are the children of God we cannot come down from the cross that proves our faith and our love.

TEMPTATION

'Thou shalt worship the Lord thy God, and Him only shalt thou serve.'
S. MATT. iv. 10

THE first temptation brings before us the suggestion that the power of which we feel conscious may be used for our own ends. It is a common experience of life that the realization of power brings with it the suggestion to use that power selfishly. The first stirrings of sex-consciousness are often accompanied by the urge just to get pleasure from that consciousness. The knowledge of power that comes to an individual or a party is often accompanied by the suggestion to use that power for the glory of the individual or some party end. But if, as children of God, we recognize that the end of our life is His glory, then we shall want as individuals to bring our sex-consciousness and every other personal power to Him for consecration and direction, and prefer, if we are members of a political party, the good of our country and the coming of the kingdom of God to any party success.

The second temptation was the suggestion that something suicidal must be an expression of faith and could claim the blessing of God. But the pure worship of the will of our Father will only lead us to a cross if His will is the way of the cross. A self-chosen cross would be as futile as the bearing of a God-appointed cross is splendid.

The third temptation suggests that success will consist in the capture and not the conversion of the world. There would be little profit in the children of men crowding the Church of God unless thereby they became the children of God. The purpose of the season of Lent is not to get crowds into churches but souls into heaven.

THE PROLOGUE AND THE EPILOGUE

'Praying always with all prayer and supplication in the Spirit, and watching thereunto with all perseverance.'—EPH. vi. 18

EVERY vocation has a prologue and an epilogue. The prologue to the apostles' vocation was their own spiritual endeavour and their reaction to the teaching of S. John the Baptist and to the expectancy in the atmosphere of those wonderful days : the epilogue was in their final faithfulness when they came back again in faith to the Master Whom they had forsaken. In our Lord's life there was the prologue to His ministry in the carpenter's shop, and the epilogue of the Passion to be the seal of His faithfulness.

Before any one of us definitely and deliberately accepted Jesus as Lord and Leader there was a prologue of preparation. Calls and crashes do not really come suddenly. The call comes as the climax to a long time of preparation : the crash comes as a climax to a long time of unfaithfulness. The epilogue is the commentary on the content of the whole life. The apostles forsook our Lord and fled, but that was not the end of the story. The epilogue shows them faithful witnesses to Him, and tells them of an inward power and peace which is deeper than the surface raging of storms.

Life brings to our discipleship a new vocation, to which what has gone before has been a prologue ; it is the vocation to go with Jesus up to Jerusalem. To come to Him first is a vocation and a prologue ; to go on with Him to Jerusalem, risking all, is the fulfilling of the vocation. If in our Jerusalem experience we should fail, as His apostles failed Him, may God grant that there may be the epilogue which will show us mellowed and humbled but still faithful, more faithful than we have ever been and going on to greater faithfulness still.

SPOKES IN A WHEEL

'Ye are My friends.'—S. John xv. 14

The highest revelation we have is a revelation of friendship. The most beautiful thing this world has ever known is the sacrifice of the ideal Friend. Our Lord revealed in the crucible of the Passion the rare gold of His friendship, as a man with His God, as a man with other men and women, as God with His creatures.

Our Lord has shown us that the relationship God covets with us is a relation of friendship. True friendship sees the friend's point of view, and understands the secrets of his heart. Some people make sex the foundation of life. Love is the foundation of life ; sex should be the channel of love. The unmarried can still let their love express itself in strength and tenderness ; so love lifts sex to highest friendship, and sex does not smirch love with any lowering.

Our relationship to one another is a revelation of our relationship to God. The perfect friendship will be born of our intercourse with God. We cannot really know another in himself, we can only know another in Christ. All our union depends on the union of each one of us with Him. As we get nearer to Him, we get nearer to each other : as we get away from Him, we get away from each other. We are like spokes in a wheel—if we are going to meet, we can only meet in the centre. A spoke, if it had eyes, could only see the outside of another spoke. If it is going to meet the other, it must travel by its own line of communication to the centre. The solving of all social and international problems will only come as the spokes of the great wheel of life meet in Christ, Who stands at its real centre.

THE SPOILT CHILDREN OF GOD

' He answered her not a word.'—S. MATT. xv. 23

THOSE words come right in the middle of the Gospel of Love, and we cannot shirk facing them. Here is a poor woman, not asking anything for herself but for another, and Jesus answers her not a word.

The Curé d'Ars used to call himself *L'enfant gâté du bon Dieu*, and his was a life of great suffering. Those who are really in the highest sense the spoilt children of God are those who are given grace to follow in the footsteps of the crucified Christ. Sometimes God has taken His dear ones out of their difficulties, but the greatest grace of God is when He enables them to go on in those difficulties. S. Paul besought Him three times that the ' thorn in the flesh ' might be taken from him, and then got the answer, ' My grace is sufficient for thee : for My strength is made perfect in weakness.' To those who are capable of rising highest in the spiritual life God gives the grace to follow Christ along the way of sorrows.

To this poor woman, who is a type, He gave grace to go on and to persevere in believing, to persevere in following, and then she got the gracious answer, ' O woman, great is thy faith : be it unto thee even as thou wilt,' and her daughter was made whole in that hour. He Who had answered not a word now answered in love and compassion, and the prayer that seemed not to be answered had its complete and perfect answer in the absolute healing of her child. Great faith is not the faith that walks always in the light and knows no darkness, but the faith that perseveres in spite of God's seeming silences, and that faith will most certainly and surely get its true reward.

TIME AND ETERNITY

'This is the will of God, even your sanctification.'—I THESS. iv. 3

IF we are not in eternity now, we never shall be. Time is the illusion ; eternity is the reality. 'The will of God is our sanctification,' says S. Paul ; 'God is Love,' says S. John. The will of Love, then, is our sanctification, and Love that is pure time cannot touch.

God does not make favourites, nor does He interfere with the laws of the universe for the private benefit of individuals. But it is His will that things and circumstances should become processes by which out of the stuff of ordinary humanity saints are formed. It is not the will of God that because of bad drains typhoid fever should become prevalent, but it is His will that doctor or priest should love patient or parishioner better than life, and so, if in going where love calls him a man meets death, he need not think that it was God's will that he should die, but he may be sure that it was God's will that he should love, and can know that death does not matter very much.

The will of God did not interfere with the free will of any man who opposed himself to Christ, nor did that will make magical things happen to remove any of the pains and difficulties that beset Him, but it was the will of God in the Resurrection of our Lord to make manifest the immortality of the Divine Love that had never for one moment wavered from its perfect end.

In our own lives many things may happen contrary to the will of God, but if we keep our wills in perfect union with His will these alien things, like the instruments of the Passion, become creative, ministering to the glory of God and the fulfilment of our own spiritual destiny.

THE PRINCIPLES OF OUR LORD'S LIFE

'Christ also hath loved us, and hath given Himself for us an offering and a sacrifice to God.'—EPH. v. 2

OUR Lord's life was made up of two ruling principles, devotion to His Father in perfect self-oblation and charity towards men. There is no rivalry between the love of God and the love of man, if both are kept in their right proportion. It was because God so loved us that Christ came, and in all His devotion to our interests and our salvation He was fulfilling and expressing His Father's will.

Our Lord never sought a cross or a mortification as ends in themselves. His way was always to follow the will of the Father in simplicity. Wherever that took Him He went, though it took Him right past His Mother to Calvary, right away from Bethany and His friends, right up to the hill of suffering He never thought of Himself in any way, either to get anything or to refuse anything. We should let things come to us in the way of the will of God, without scruple and without presumption, accepting them if they come, not coveting them if they do not. ' Ask nothing—refuse nothing ' was a maxim of S. Francis de Sales.

To live in love and charity with our neighbours is not easy, and for no one can it have been more difficult than for our Lord. No one could have seen the limitations of others more clearly than our Lord did or been more conscious of their sinfulness, but He lived in love and charity with them, and was Himself the principle of unity that brought them together.

At the Crucifixion these two principles are set forth very manifestly. We see there the supreme self-oblation of our Lord's perfect devotion to His Father and His perfect charity to men.

33

THE TROUBLED HEART

'Let not your heart be troubled.'—S. JOHN xiv. 1

SURELY if any men had a right to have troubled hearts, it was the men to whom these words were first spoken. First of all, they had come to be dependent upon the manifest presence of Jesus, and over them was the shadow of the approaching withdrawal of that presence. Then they had seen a vision of the kingdom of God, but it seemed as though the kingdom of this world would prove the stronger. Also they had lost confidence in themselves through a sense of insecurity which came from their fear of their own unfaithfulness.

We may ask ourselves whether there has ever been a time when these three things have not in some measure or degree seemed to threaten the life of the Church. Do we not know sometimes what it is to feel as though Jesus had left us ? and does not materialism often seem to triumph over spiritual things ? and do we not recognize in ourselves, and in many who hold office in the Church of God, that which would cause us to echo the words of the Psalmist : ' Put not your trust in princes, nor in any child of man : for there is no help in them ' ? Yet down through the ages the voice of the Master sounds : ' Let not your heart be troubled.'

He spoke those words as He Himself passed into the agony and darkness of the night, and, if we will believe in the truth of His majestic utterance, in the degree that we remain in union with Him, we shall know His experience, and go with faith through whatever dark night there may be, certain of the resurrection that waits beyond.

THE WILL AND THE WAY

'Ye believe in God.'—S. John xiv. i

If we believe in God, that which we say about ourselves must be peculiarly true of Him—'Where there's a will, there's a way.' God has an eternal purpose for His creation, and it must be true that He has a way to bring about the realization of that purpose, and Calvary shows us to what length He will go to accomplish His end. In a charming story of S. Teresa we are told that some one asked her how much she had got towards her new convent. He was told twopence. 'You can't do much on twopence,' said her questioner. 'No,' replied S. Teresa, 'I can't, but God can.' We can be quite certain, if we really believe in God, that the victory must remain with God. A defeated God would not be God.

Three things are surely very clear to us about ourselves. First, there is in us a great darkness. How little any one of us knows about himself, his neighbour, the world, or God. Secondly, we are conscious of absolute weakness. Left to ourselves, we do the wrong thing again and again. Thirdly, we know what it is to be completely lonely. To those men who were so soon to find out these three things about themselves, their darkness, their weakness, their utter loneliness, the great Master said, 'Ye believe in God.' We believe in God. We turn from our darkness to His light ; and He will not only give us light, but also the power to follow the light ; and when we are alone, we may learn that we are least alone, because our God and Father, the Father of our Lord Jesus Christ, is with us.

MAN'S FAILURE : GOD'S SUCCESS

'Believe also in Me.'—S. JOHN xiv. 1

WHERE there 's a will, there 's a way, and these words of our Lord remind us that He is God's way. God's will is God's love, and the will and the way of God are interpreted in the Incarnation and Passion of our Lord. We have believed in ourselves and our own way and have done our own will, and it has all ended in failure. The Divine Master, Who reveals the will and the way of God, stands before us, and says, ' Believe in Me.'

As we believe in Him, let us draw nearer to Him in penitence, learning from Him the things about which we should be penitent. If we are not conscious of sin, it is due to one of two reasons : one, that the perfection and beauty of Christ has not fully dawned upon us ; and the other, that our sense of sin has been dulled by sin. Penitence is not a morbid thing ; it just means being teachable. A man who thinks he has nothing to learn makes it quite impossible for any one to teach him

As we kneel in penitence, let us hear His voice saying to us in love and pity, ' Believe in Me. I am here to forgive you, I am here to help you, I am here to be your comrade along the way.' As we draw near to Him in prayer, let us hear His voice saying, ' Believe in Me. I know what you would say before you say it. I am here to give you My peace : let not your heart be troubled.' As we come to Him in Holy Communion, let us hear Him saying, ' Believe in Me. I am here to give you Myself.' That is the voice of the Son of God, the Saviour of men.

THE STRONG SON OF GOD

'Stronger than he.'—S. LUKE xi. 22

CHRISTIANITY is a religion of strength, and Christ is the strong Son of God, stronger than the strongest. We want to make our religion a real thing. It is not just filling a pew on Sunday or coming to a festival. Our religion ought to be, and is, if it is real, a tremendous conflict. We have often to go down on our knees and say, ' I am not going to get up till I have won a spiritual victory. Here is a strong man holding me by the throat, but there is One stronger than he, and he is going to be laid low.'

The poor man at Gadara, possessed by a legion of devils, was a terror to himself and the countryside. He was possessed by fear, but there came One stronger than his fear, stronger than his darkness and disease. Jesus without any fear went to him, and told him that he was the child of God, and, as we last get a glimpse of that man, he is clothed and in his right mind, and, instead of being the terror, he is the evangelist of the countryside. He is preparing the way for the mission that Jesus will take when He comes to Gadara again.

There is that mysterious possession of evil, which we call the devil. We have all of us known what it is to be gripped by some unreasoning passion, some unreasoning hatred, something of which we say, ' This thing is not me, though it seeks to possess me.' This mysterious power of evil exists. ' While men slept,' the ' enemy sowed tares among the wheat.' But there is a power stronger than the enemy, the strong man, Christ our Saviour.

THE SOUL OF JESUS CRUCIFIED

'He hath made Him to be sin for us, Who knew no sin; that we might be made the righteousness of God in Him.'—2 COR. V. 21

IF we are to die to self and live to God, we must have a principle set before us and a method to follow. This is set before us in the lifting up of the standard of the Cross. Not only the beauty of the Sacred Infancy but the wonder of the Passion must be our vision.

If we think of the soul of Jesus as He hangs on the Cross, it is the same soul as praised the Father at Nazareth, but it has gone through all the experience of the three-and-thirty years. Every thought of His had been in accordance with the will of God from the time that He was conceived of the Holy Ghost till this time of His supreme obedience, and yet the reward of that obedience is to be nailed to the Cross and to meet the temptation to question whether the suffering were worth while. We can only hold on to the two parallel truths, that the soul of Jesus was never separated from God, and that His soul was plunged into unutterable darkness. He was made sin for us that we might know the righteousness of God in Him. The height of His knowledge and the depth of His love made the measure of His agony.

In the measure in which we are trying to become sons of God, we shall know union with the pain of the soul of Jesus. The more we love, the more we know, and the more we suffer in union with Him. The moment of His supreme victory was preceded by a moment of supreme anguish, and only so can the soul follow His soul to eternal life. Day by day we are to learn more of the soul of Jesus crucified.

THE LIGHT OF THE WORLD

'I am the Light of the World.'—S. JOHN ix. 5

THE sun is the source of material light, and all light comes from it. In the same way all spiritual light, the light of beauty of thought, of purity of love, of goodness in people everywhere, has come from the one source of light, which is God. We have the power of assimilating light, but we cannot of ourselves create light. If our eyes are normal, we can use the light though we cannot ourselves provide it. So we have spiritual eyes to see what is beautiful and fair, but we have not in ourselves the power of creating light.

Jesus is the Light of the World. He has taken a human nature and in that human nature He has set the light of the Divine Nature, so revealing what human nature was meant for. It was meant for this great end, that in it should shine the Divine Light. When we look at our Lord, we see a humanity which is utterly lovely and perfectly pure, and yet so completely human that to Him went those two types who more than any other cry out for what is human, the sinner and the child.

If people have bad eyes, they cannot stand the light. It is not the fault of the light, it is the fault of their eyes. If people do not love Jesus, it is always because they have had some wrong impression of Him, or because in some way their organs of spiritual vision have become diseased. God has given the light of the sun to bless our eyes, and the light of His dear Son to bless our souls, the true Light which shines upon every man.

GRASPING AND GIVING

'Let this mind be in you, which was also in Christ Jesus.'—PHIL. ii. 5

THE words in Philippians ii. 6, ' He thought it not robbery to be equal with God,' would be better translated, ' thought it not a thing to be grasped at to be equal with God.' The sin of Adam was that he thought it a thing to be grasped at to be equal with God ; the greatness of God consists in this, that *He* could think it a thing to be grasped at to be equal in experience with poor, tempted men and women in every difficulty, pain, and temptation that they can know. The prodigal son in the parable thought it a thing to be grasped at to have all his money to spend ; Christ in His Passion thought it a thing to be grasped at to spend His life in revealing the love of God to sinners, and to spend it where He could most lavishly, upon the Cross.

If we get quietly down upon our knees before our crucifix and think this out, how our sense of values begins to alter ! The word ' grasp ' begins to go, and the word ' give ' begins to take its place. We see how often ' other gods ' have sat upon the throne of our wills. When we are possessed by some grasping desire, it really means that God is not reigning in our lives. A real repentance means dethroning this grasping spirit which has suggested to us that we are the centre of the circle, and enthroning the Christ spirit which only asks to be equal with the last sufferer in the opportunity of suffering, to be equal with the most tempted in the opportunity of bearing temptation, to win to such a place in life's experience as shall allow of no other ever saying to Him, ' I suffered something that you never knew.'

A DAILY DYING

'As Christ was raised up from the dead by the glory of the Father, even so we also should walk in newness of life.'—Rom. vi. 4

S. Paul often tells the readers of his Epistles that by Baptism they die to an old life and rise to a new life in Christ, and that this new life is to have for its inspiration the glorious Resurrection life of our Lord. We know that our religion does not end at the Cross. If it did, it would be a very sad affair. The whole reason of our Lord's death was that there might be life more abundant.

We have to try to die with our Lord if we would rise with Him. Our Lord's life was in a mystical sense a daily dying. There came the day when He completely died, in darkness, shame, and pain, and in proportion to the completeness of His death was the completeness and the perfection of His Resurrection.

All of us have some particular weakness of our own, a quick temper, laziness, or some kind of selfishness. It is to this we must learn to die daily, if we would live the new life in Christ. If we allow our bodies by their desires to dull our devotion and obscure our spiritual vision, then we live to the flesh and die to Christ, but if we keep them in subjection, then we die to the flesh and live to Christ.

We must die to our own self-will. The reason we do things should be because we believe them to be in harmony with the will of God. We must die to our own self-love. The saints have always been at peace within themselves, because they have never thought about themselves. Only out of the death of self-love can there be a resurrection to the love of God.

SPIRITUAL DARKNESS

'I had fainted, unless I had believed to see the goodness of the Lord in the land of the living.'—Ps. xxvii. 13

IF we would reach the highest perfection, we must be ready, as all the saints tell us, to die to spiritual consolations. There is bound to come a time, in the experience of a soul that God is going to make perfect, when it has no consciousness of its own peace or love, but only a great hunger and weariness ; no consciousness of its faith, which yet alone keeps it going on, but only of darkness and spiritual distress, or, what is perhaps even worse, spiritual boredom. Like her Lord, the soul is now entering into the dark sanctuary of sacrifice, and becoming like Him at once priest and victim.

A great Frenchman, Père Grou, writes : ' A time comes when God will take away all spiritual consolations from a soul. No more has she a taste for anything. Everything weighs on her, everything bores her, everything fatigues her. No longer does she feel the presence of God in herself. She has peace, but she does not even know it. She does not even believe that she has it. It is necessary that the soul be generous, that she consents to these privations, that she accustoms herself to seek for nothing, to love quite purely, and to serve Him for Himself at her own expense.'

If we have to go through a time of great darkness and weariness, let us never think that is a sign that we are forsaken by God or necessarily in a bad spiritual condition. It *may* be due to some refusal of union with the will of God, but it may just be part of our spiritual education, a death to emotion and in the sphere of the senses, that there may be a resurrection of the will and a new life in the sphere of the pure love of God.

LYING IN STATE

*'He took upon Him the form of a servant . . . and became
obedient unto death.'*—PHIL. ii. 7, 8

WE read constantly in the papers of the queue of people who
file by the coffin of some great personage who lies in state
in abbey or cathedral. The poor body lies there, cased in
oak, draped and beflowered, surrounded by burning tapers ;
the soul, however good the man may have been, is but the
soul of a creature, who has probably learnt through life's
schooling to say with sincerity the prayer of the Publican,
' God be merciful to me a sinner.'

How different was the scene at the close of our Lord's
life ! Let us pass by the Cross in single file, and take a long
look at Him Who hangs there   Our Lord's body hung then
in the place of shame, without the walls of the Holy City,
upon a rough cross that had been knocked together carelessly
by some poorly-paid executioners, excommunicate, com-
panioned with two criminals. Such was the outward
semblance of things then.

But if the veil of appearances that hangs between us and
reality could have been lifted, what a difference there would
have been between the lying in state of a human king and of
Him Who on Calvary bore the form of a servant. The
exterior surroundings of the earthly king would have been
the funeral pomp and pageantry considered by his subjects
appropriate to the occasion : the interior condition of the
soul would have been that of a creature before his Creator.
The strange exterior ritual of Calvary veiled the radiant
triumph of the soul of Jesus and the victory of His Sacred
Humanity. If one authentic inch of the rough wood of His
Cross could now be held by human fingers, no shrine would
be deemed fair enough to furnish its resting-place.

THE WITNESS OF THE RESURRECTION

'This Jesus hath God raised up, whereof we all are witnesses.'
ACTS ii. 32

IT is an unthinkable supposition that a life so apparently ordinary and a death so common as our Lord's could have been preached as a Gospel and proclaimed by a few poor peasants and had any weight of witness, unless these men had been transfigured by a living faith. Unlettered men could not have faced the might of Rome and the intellect of Greece, unless they had been upheld by an experience to them so certainly true that no other kind of experience could shake it and bring a reaction of disillusionment.

Again, when one authentic relic of Christ's body would have proved for ever that the story of His Resurrection was untrue, it is impossible to suppose that that relic would not have been procured if it had been possible. Every murder trial reveals how difficult it is to get rid of a body, when there is every reason to do so. In the case of our Lord's body, all the actors in the drama wished to produce it : His friends to pay it honour, His enemies as a proof that He had not risen. There can be no explanation of the empty tomb except that the Church's faith in the Resurrection is true.

But our belief in the living Christ is something much more than just belief in His survival after death. There is nothing necessarily divine in that. Our Lord's death was the consummation of His perfect obedience to the divine law of love, which is the eternal will of His heavenly Father. What from the earthly side of things looked like death and failure, from the heavenly side of things was manifest as the perfect victory of love. His death was the revelation of Eternal Love, which His Resurrection revealed to be Eternal Life.

44

THE EFFECT OF THE RESURRECTION

*'Let us run with patience the race that is set before us, looking
unto Jesus.'*—HEB. xii. 1, 2

ONE of the most cogent arguments for the truth of our Lord's
Resurrection is the effect it produced in the apostles. These
men, who had all fled away at the Crucifixion, gathered
courage such as they had never had when they had His
actual living presence with them, courage which enabled
them to meet martyrdom, and power to preach the Gospel of
Christ and convince others. It is inconceivable that these
poor frightened men could have gained this courage and power
for any reason but the reason they themselves alleged, that
they had contact with their living Lord.

But they gained something more, an understanding of our
Lord's character and nature, which we see growing and
growing in their letters, the Epistles. The men who had
expected that He would bring down fire on the Samaritans
who did not give Him a welcome, whose idea of the Kingdom
was a kingdom in which they would sit on His right hand and
His left, were learning more and more the mind of Christ.
Our Lord never worked a miracle for display or as an argument for His divinity, and after His Resurrection He did not
appear in all His glory to those who had condemned Him
and tread them under His feet. The apostles learnt the
mind of their Master in His Resurrection as in His life,
that it was not just by rising from the dead that His divinity
was proved, but by His life of love and holiness. They
realized that by that very way in which He revealed Himself
they were to reveal Him, by the way of love rather than by
miracles, and they went forth determined to serve Him in
the way of sacrifice, lowliness, and service.

THE UNCOMMON IN THE COMMON

'Is not this the carpenter?'—S. MARK vi. 3

WE are so used to our own especial veneration of the Holy Cross that we are inclined to think of our Lord's Life and Death as extraordinary in their setting as well as in their holiness. This is not the case. The wonder of our Lord's Life and Death is not that they are extraordinary, but that a life lived in so ordinary a setting, and a death died in so common a shame, should have shined with such a far-reaching radiance, and should be continuing to shine until surely at the last every sort of slavery and worship of violence will be shamed out of existence by the influence of its healing beauty.

Our Lord never travelled further than the distance between London and York. He followed the common trade of a carpenter, He died a death that many another died, and the whole length of His earthly life was just three-and-thirty years, the whole duration of His active ministry not more than three. When He said, ' If any one will come after Me, let him take up his cross and follow Me,' He was alluding to the quite common sight of a batch of men, condemned to be crucified, going to the place of execution in procession, following the leader carrying his cross. Many a man died on a cross ; many a mother, many a friend stood by the crucified. Calvaries were quite common in those cruel days.

It is the very commonness of the occasion, the very unbelievableness of the ensuing marvel, the far-reaching permanence of the influence of the Resurrection, that add their threefold weight of evidence to the experience of the Christian believer of intercourse with the living Christ in prayer and sacrament.

THE CHALLENGE OF FAITH

'How long halt ye between two opinions ? if the Lord be God, follow Him : but if Baal, then follow him.'—1 KINGS xviii. 21

IN this ancient story Elijah, the man of faith, challenges the people to challenge God. He sets his sacrifice on the altar and says : ' Drench it with water, and make it absolutely certain that no natural flame can possibly set it alight, so that if a flame is seen on that altar it shall be sure and certain that the flame is the flame of God.'

Now let us look at a second picture, which we have had before us in Holy Week, when it seems as if God Himself challenges the people to drench His Sacrifice not with water but with blood. His Sacrifice is the Sacrifice of Himself. ' Drench Me with pain,' He seems to say. ' Cast Me out, forsaken and rejected, and see if the Father will save Me.' On the lonely hill of Calvary the Lord was seen rejected, defeated, accursed ; in the natural sphere we cannot imagine any completer failure than the failure of Christ. But as in the ancient story the divine fire did come, and revealed that the sacrifice of Elijah was the sacrifice that was accepted of God, so the divine glory of the Resurrection descended upon that rejected Figure, to prove that that which looked so like a defeat was really Love's completest victory.

So with the thought of Elijah's drenched sacrifice nevertheless consumed by fire, with the thought of the defeated Christ nevertheless glorious and radiant in the Garden of the Resurrection, let us be sure and certain that Truth can never fail, that Love must triumph, and that we who are the children of God are the children of the Resurrection and are already beginning to live the everlasting life.

FOUNDATIONS

'Therefore whosoever heareth these sayings of Mine, and doeth them, I will liken him unto a wise man, which built his house upon a rock.'
S. MATT. vii. 24

ALL of us are builders. We are building the house of our lives around us, and builders are responsible people. Some houses fit into the landscape and are an addition to the scenery, and some mar the countryside. Lives may bring comfort and charm, or distress and trouble. Then the houses of our lives are meant to be different. There is nothing so dull as seeing an interminable number of houses exactly alike. We have to build our particular houses according to our temperaments and the gifts God has given us. God grant that we may not be building ugly structures that may offend the divine eye or chill the pilgrim soul that passes.

In our Lord's story there were two houses, one built upon the sand and the other upon the rock. They were probably quite different houses to look at, but that is not the point. They were built on different foundations, and a storm came on both of them, and one house stood and the other fell. The difference was not in the house or the storm, but in the foundation. The tempest of life will show what we are built upon. If we are built on the rock of the Faith, the house we build will never be overcome by the troubles and temptations of life.

Our Lord Himself built the house of His life upon the rock of faith in the Divine Love. What a humble house it was ! If we think of our Lord in any setting, it is always a humble setting—the lowly bed in the manger, the simple outdoor life, the carpenter's shop. Think how the storm of life beat on Christ's house. Calvary gives us the measure of the storm. Easter represents to us how that house weathered the storm.

THE BUILDING OF THE HOUSE

'It was founded upon a rock.'—S. MATT. vii. 25

WE want to build up every room of the house of our life upon the one foundation of our holy Faith.

We may have a guest-chamber, and we think all the guests who come there are true and splendid. Then one day a guest robs us or disappoints us terribly. Is that bit of our house going to crumble? It will, if it is not built on the foundation of our faith in Christ. Perhaps we have our chapel, where we gather with those we love. Then some friend deserts the Church, or somebody we believed to be exceedingly pious and good turns out to be extraordinarily human, perhaps to have fallen into some grave fault. Is this chapel of our faith going to tumble down? It will, if it is not built upon the true rock of Christ. Then we have our hobby room, where we do the things we like doing. Is that room going to be so big and take up so much of our time that there will not be room for anything else? That will happen unless our foundation is Jesus.

But all these different rooms of the house of our life may be built on the one foundation. Then they will make up a harmonious whole, and none of them will be broken down by the storm. A friend may be untrue, the Church may seem to fail us; but we will never be untrue to our friend or our Church. We may love our work or our hobbies, but we shall be able to keep them consecrated. The storm will beat on our guest-chamber, our private chapel, our hobby room; but all these things will stand, if they are built upon the foundation of faith in our Lord Jesus Christ.

THE CHRIST IN THE CHRISTIAN

'Andrew and Philip tell Jesus.'—S. JOHN xii. 22

EVEN as Philip and Andrew represented Jesus those long years ago, people have a right to say to you and me, ' Sir, we would see Jesus.' Worldly cynicism about the Church is really the echo of the spiritual hunger that cries, ' We would see Jesus.' The doubting pathetic world, longing for light and peace, seeks to find some authentic trace of Christ in the lives and conversation of those who call themselves Christians.

We can only do what Philip and Andrew did, go and tell Jesus. Here comes the call to the life of prayer. Let us go to Him and say, ' Master, the people in our street are asking to see You, and we are utterly unfit to tell them about You, to deliver Your message. We bring their needs to You.' The professing Church can only go to Jesus with that cry, and try to learn from Him. When those apostles went to Him with the cry of the Greeks, He talked to them about His Passion (*S. John* xii. 23–35). He said, ' Now is the Son of Man glorified,' and what was the glory ? The glory of the Cross! He spoke then the parable of the corn of wheat and the life dependent upon the death, and referred it to Himself and that lifting up of the Passion which would alone draw all men to Him. We have to learn the secret of the Passion, that, if we would draw all men to Jesus by our lives, it will only be if these lives of ours are sacramentally united with His Sacrifice and expressed in a love that will go on loving through all things, in a forgiveness unto seventy times seven, and a heroic faith that can follow through any darkness.

LEARNING AND KNOWING

'If ye had known Me, ye should have known My Father also.'

S. JOHN xiv. 7

S. PHILIP is the saint of quest and of spiritual hunger. He longs to know. ' Show us the Father,' is his cry to our Lord. The beloved disciple was a person who revelled in facts. The translators of our Bible have rendered two entirely different Greek words by the same English word, ' know.' The first is always used by S. John when he is speaking of our knowledge : the second when he is speaking of our Lord's knowledge. The first kind of knowledge expresses the learning gained by a student, the second represents the intuition of the artist, who sees a thing and grasps the whole significance of it. There is a sense of uncertainty and incompleteness about the first word, a complete certainty expressed in the second. To bring out the full meaning of this text one might paraphrase it, ' If ye had been learning Me, ye would have been arriving at a certain knowledge of My Father.'

The Bible is really the guided, inspired word of man about the Word of God, but there is only one real Word of God, and that is our Lord Jesus Christ. The Bible gives us the inspired prophecy that looks forward to His coming, and the inspired memoirs of men who wrote about Him when He came, but the one Word of God that abideth for ever is our Lord Jesus Christ. He is the everlasting Word that shall never fail, He is the everlasting revelation that shall never pass away, the everlasting Life in Whom alone we shall find our perfect peace.

THE SCHOOL OF LIFE

'He that loveth not knoweth not God ; for God is Love.'

I S. JOHN iv. 8

LIFE is a school, in which we are to learn to know God, and we learn to know God by learning to love. That is the great end of life. Life is an opportunity for learning to love. God is Love. Our Lord said, ' I am the Way, and the Truth, and the Life.' He reveals the Way of love, the Truth about love, and *is* the Life because He is Love. That is what we have to learn to know. There is little point in learning to be great experts about theology, or knowing all about the ritual of the Church, if we have not learnt to love one another and how to love even those who do us wrong.

The great examination we all have to go through is the examination of the Cross. In the school of God we do not go to a place where we are asked questions and try to write down some answer. God has willed that life itself should be the examination, and the things that come upon us are the questions that are set. In other words, each of us has his cross, and the cross is the examination which is to prove whether we have learnt to love, and the reward is the power to love perfectly. That is the great prize we are to get out of life, and only if we love perfectly shall we be able to see God, because it is only love that can see love and understand love. If we learn in the school of life the wondrous secret of love, we shall see God and behold the vision of His beauty.

THE BODY OF CHRIST

'The Church, which is His body.'—EPH. i. 22, 23

THESE words are much more than a figure of speech. They contain a very great idea. A body is that through which a mind functions, through which a soul operates. The Church, the Body of Christ, like any other body, has a function, a function *in* the world, *to* the world, and *for* the world. There are three ways of regarding the relationship of the Church and the world.

Some people look upon religion as something altogether apart from the world, and the Church as a place of escape from the world That is one way of looking at it. You enter into the Church and save your own soul, and do not care at all about the world.

Another way of looking at the world is as a battle-ground, in which character is made. There is no real relation between the Church and the world, but we have to endure things in the world for the formation of our characters.

The third and right thought is that the function of the Church is to restore God's order in this world. The world is meant to be the revelation of the will of God, and sin came and destroyed the order. Then our Lord came, and ordained and founded the Church, which is His Body, to restore God's order in the world. The function of the Church is to bring about a right fulfilment of the will of God. In the Incarnation we see the Body of Christ *in* the world, showing forth healing and comfort *to* the world, and offered *for* the world in perfect sacrifice. The Church of God is meant to be *in* the world, shedding forth light and love and healing *to* the world, and offering its continual prayer and sacrifice *for* the world.

SPIRITUAL EDUCATION

'Ye know not what ye ask.'—S. MATT. xx. 22

IT is well for us to consider the education of the spiritual life. James and John had to learn, as Peter had to learn, the kind of Christ they believed in. Peter cried, 'Thou art the Christ, the Son of the living God,' but when our Lord began to speak to him of the Sacred Passion, to tell of the Cross and the agony and shame and apparent defeat, then S. Peter said, 'That be far from Thee, Lord,' and he who had been called Peter one minute was called Satan the next. When Salome asked that her two sons might be on our Lord's right hand and His left, she had a vision of splendid royalty. The vision of the cup of a king in an oriental woman's mind was the golden cup brought by a cupbearer at a banquet, when the king was celebrating some great victory. Neither Salome nor James nor John could dream what the cup of our Lord really was. They knew not what they asked, nevertheless what they asked was granted them.

Every time we say the Lord's Prayer we pray, 'Thy will be done,' and indeed we know not what we ask. Every time we come to our communion we drink the cup of His Precious Blood, and we know not for what that grace is given to us, what challenge is coming to every part of our being. We know not what the will of God is going to be in our lives, but we do know this, that the will of God is that *our* will should be one with *His* will, and that when we drink of His cup and receive the communion of His Sacred Body we should take into our beings the power of the everlasting love of God.

TRAVAIL

'Your sorrow shall be turned into joy.'—S. JOHN xvi. 20

In the context of this passage our Lord spoke about a mother's travail. If we think Who spoke this word 'travail,' and when, it is a word very full of teaching and significance. It was God interpreting divine wisdom through human nature Who spoke this word on the eve of His Passion.

A woman in travail is in pain, because her hour is come. When her child is born into the world, she laughs for joy and forgets her pain, because that has been born which could only come through pain. That agony through which Christ went was not a death throe but a travail pang. We could never have seen the loveliness of the love of God, if it had not been for the travail pangs of the Passion.

We may have to go through very difficult times, but through those difficulties a better man, a better woman, may be born. Life is ours to put into it the best we have to give, and we must believe that out of the travail that comes from that self-surrender, that self-discipline, a man shall be born who is worthy of the great God Who willed to come to us by the way of the Manger and leave us by the way of the Cross. As we think of life and its difficulties, it will make all the difference whether we think of its pains as death throes or travail pangs. The parable of the mother, who goes down to the valley of the shadow of death that her child may walk in the sun and know the experience of life, was precious to our Lord. To Him the pain of life was not a death throe ending in a grave, but a travail pang, the prelude to a fuller life.

GLIMPSES

*'A little while, and ye shall not see Me : and again, a little while,
and ye shall see Me, because I go to the Father.'*—S. JOHN xvi. 16

THESE words sum up the interior experience of most Christians. We are led to God by glimpses. What glimpses of God
we get in the New Testament ! First, a little Babe in the
Manger. Then we do not see Him for a long time, till we
see a Boy in the Temple hearing and asking questions.
Then after a long time we get more glimpses : a Man working in a carpenter's shop—in the wilderness in an agony of
temptation—asleep in a boat on the lake—on a mountain
in a wonderful night of prayer.

Is it not our experience that our spiritual life has just
been glimpses of Christ in the same sort of way ? In our
early days we see the simplicity of Christ, the beauty of the
Babe. Then perhaps there comes a time of darkness, when
we do not see Him at all. Then we get a glimpse of Him
as the tempted Christ, and we begin to see that the temptations
and trials of life are the opportunities of life. Again, for a
little while we do not see Him, and then the Christ of the
carpenter's shop reveals Himself, and we begin to find that
just the day's work is comradeship with Him. Then perhaps again He passes out of sight, and we have to learn that
in the sufferings of life we are getting glimpses of the pain
of God.

We have to make up our minds to periods of darkness
in the spiritual life. It must have been terribly hard for the
apostles to hear the words, ' It is expedient for you that I
go away.' But they passed from glimpses of the risen Christ
during the great forty days following the Resurrection to the
indwelling possession of the Holy Spirit.

THE BURDEN-BEARER

'We then that are strong ought to bear the infirmities of the weak.'

ROM. xv. 1

IN the delightful legend of S. Christopher we are told how the simple giant made up his mind that he would only give his service to the most powerful prince in the world, and how, after trying in turn the service of a famous king and the Evil One, he set out to find the Christ, Whose Cross was more powerful than either. We all know the sequel and the eternal verities represented by the story—how other services pall before the service of Christ ; how, when one has accepted Christ, the sweet and simple Gospel may give one a very heavy burden to bear ; and yet the faithful bearing of it is the only way in which one may hope to get through to the other side of life's storms and torrents.

The Christian way of facing every problem will be by using it sacrificially and being content that all the weight of suffering should come, if need be, upon ourselves. If people come to us in trouble, we have to try to take the trouble upon ourselves. Sometimes it is a fearful weight, and that was the weight that killed our Lord. But we have to do our best to meet the difficulties of life in union with the world's great Burden-Bearer, Jesus Christ our Lord.

S. Christopher stands before us as an eternal type of the steadfast faith that will go on through the storm, of the enduring love that will bear the burden that Love lays on the shoulders of love and count it part of the vocation of Christ, of the hope that quests on ever along the way of love, however hard that way may be, till the act of human service is at last lifted to be the revelation of the Divine Communion.

A HEART AT LIBERTY

'I will run the way of Thy commandments, when Thou hast set my heart at liberty.'—Ps. cxix. 32

To say that a machine is ' running freely ' means that every part of the machine is performing its function. When there is a bit of grit somewhere, the mechanic says, ' The machine is not running freely. There is something wrong. I must overhaul it.' Now something has got into human nature, a bit of grit, and it has not been running freely. We find opposition in ourselves : one part of us opposes another part. Our nature is not functioning freely in all its parts. Part of us would grasp at something, and part would condemn the desire. Human nature is not in perfect harmony with its Creator, and because of that we have not liberty to run in the way of God's commandments, because of the entry of this evil thing, this bit of grit which we call sin.

Many of us have a completely wrong idea of what is meant by freedom. S. Paul asked his converts to remember the words of our Lord Jesus Christ, Who said that it was more blessed to give than to receive. The world thinks it much better to receive than to give, and all of us are tempted to think like that. But when we are truly getting through to God in prayer, then we are able to think rightly about these things. When we get down on our knees and try to be still, we feel, ' I do so want to give myself, and I can't do it.' We long to give, and all the while there is something fighting us and making us want to get. The conquest of this desire to get, the coming into being and true dominance of the desire to give, is the attaining to that liberty which is the true liberty of the children of God.

TRUE DEVOTION

Every good gift and every perfect gift is from above, and cometh down from the Father.'—S. JAS. i. 17

DEVOTION to God is God's own gift. It is the gift of the Holy Spirit, but it is something we have to pray for, and, since it can constantly grow, we can never think we have it in full perfection. Devotion comes from God, and is constantly returning to God, and ends in God.

True devotion is a deep interior disposition. It is something deeper than the intellect, deeper than the imagination, deeper than any emotion or feeling. It is something fixed, habitual, and permanent, which enters into every moment of life, is the foundation of every act, and the very soul of conduct. The will is captive to the will of God, and not enslaved by passion or dominated by any creature.

The secret of devotion is really in the character of our prayer. Part of prayer is just a quiet retirement into the deep of one's soul, where one may find the presence of God. As the body has a soul, so may a soul have a soul, and the true soul of our soul is the presence of God. ' The kingdom of heaven,' said our Lord, ' is within you.' The best prayer is not that which feels most, but that which gives most. In the quiet union of the two wills, the human and the divine, is the essence of true prayer.

Our salvation, thank God ! depends much more on His love of us than on our love of Him. As we read the writings of the apostles, we see how very much more they talk of God's love for them than of their love for Him. ' Neither death, nor life, nor angels, nor principalities, nor powers,' says S. Paul, ' shall be able to separate us from the love of God.'

DEVOTION TO GOD AND CREATURES

'Thou shalt love the Lord thy God with all thy heart, and with all thy soul, and with all thy mind, and with all thy strength.'

S. MARK xii. 30

DEVOTION means the expenditure of oneself and one's affection upon another person or thing. All devotion is beautiful, the devotion of a son to a mother, of a friend to a friend, of a man to his country. But there is something which marks the difference between devotion to any created person or thing and devotion to God. That great distinction is this. All devotion to creatures has to be limited and conditioned. A son cannot do *anything* for his mother : he cannot commit sin for her. No one can do *everything* for his or her friend : they must not put a creature in the place of God. The whole condition of the health of a devotion to any creature depends on that devotion being limited and conditioned. However much a man may love his country, he has no right to put the love of his country in front of the law of his God. However much a man may love his friend, his friendship has to be conditioned by the laws of God and limited by his obedience to God.

But our devotion to Almighty God depends upon its being unlimited and unconditioned. Devotion to a creature that has no limit or condition is what we call inordinate affection, but devotion to God which *is* limited and conditioned is robbed of its meaning. There is no rivalry between the love of God and the love of one's neighbour, because one's love of one's neighbour will only be a true love if it is conditioned by the love of God. The glory of God and the good of one's neighbour will be the two motives that, ever in union, control a devout life. Out of our love of God will come true social service and true love of mankind.

THE END OF DEVOTION

'Draw nigh to God, and He will draw nigh to you.'—S. JAS. iv. 8

THE end of devotion is not to become extraordinarily devout. It is possible to fill one's life with practices of piety, and yet not to get more Christ-like. It is possible to spend much time in devotion, and yet to be hard and critical and to lack a missionary and loving spirit. It is a terrible, as well as a salutary, thing to remember that it was devout people at a time of special devotion who killed our Lord.

God Himself must be the sole end of our devotion. There is no great danger of our worshipping graven images, but there is a very great danger of our worshipping mental images of our own imagining. God has been revealed to us in the dear figure of Christ, and the supreme revelation of God is a naked man dying on the gallows in the dark. We have to be dispossessed of our mental images of a sentimental Christ by this stark reality of the perfect sacrifice of the Cross. He is our model. He never thought of Himself or His own interests. He never did one single action because He was bribed in any way to do it. He never abstained from any action for fear of what might happen to Him. In all things He sought only and always His Father's will.

The end of devotion is attained when the complete taking of all things meets with the complete giving of all things. Death, the great taker, is defeated when he meets Christ, the great giver. The supreme devotion of our Lord's life was consummated as He laid down His life for His sheep and yielded His spirit in perfect faith to His Father. The true end of devotion is the gift of ourselves and all we have to God.

MEANS OF DEVOTION

'I will behave myself wisely in a perfect way.'—Ps. ci. 2

ONE help to true devotion to God will be a sensible rule of life. A rule, of course, must never be an ideal, or it may become an idol. It is not something we are trying to attain to, but something below which we will not let ourselves drop. Every one should have some note of order in his spiritual life.

Part of this rule will be a definite practice of mental prayer. We shall keep a certain time in the day when we occupy ourselves with the thought of God. We need not pray a great deal in words but simply let our minds rest upon God. By this practice we attain to a habit of recollection of the Divine Presence.

Spiritual reading, and reading spiritually, are a very true means of arriving at devotion. Sometimes in a good story we find a great deal of spiritual help. The Bible is of course the supreme classic of the spiritual life.

The principle of mortification or self-discipline, the attaining to the possession of oneself that one may give oneself to God, is a means to perfection of life. The best means of mortification are those that come without our looking for them, in the ordinary contradictions of life, which we should recognize as coming to us in the will of God, accept, consecrate, and offer.

The Sacraments are the surest means we have of doing to death our self-love and enthroning upon our wills the will of God. That is natural, as they are the means appointed by our Lord Himself.

Lastly, it is a good thing to have a director for one's soul. God has given His priests a vocation to minister to the souls of His children, and to His children a vocation to accept that direction.

ALONE

'Alone . . . yet . . . not alone.'—S. John xvi. 32

To be alone is certainly not good, and we cannot think it even of God. The God we worship is not a unit but a Unity, i.e. He has relations in Himself. To be quite lonely would be to be quite blank. When a child is afraid of being alone, it is not only loneliness it is afraid of : it is also afraid of something there. It is not alone, but accompanied by a fear.

Again, one can know very well what it is to be *not* alone and yet fearfully alone One can be tremendously lonely in the midst of a crowd. Many a one has to be alone in uncongenial circumstances, trying to witness to the truth, to stand up for Christ, to keep true to a great ideal in a hostile atmosphere, to stand up for purity in the midst of low minds and low gossip, to stand up for faith in the midst of incredulity and scathing prejudice.

But, if it is possible to be immensely alone in the midst of a crowd, it is also possible to be in wondrous sweet company in utter solitude. That is a thing that is given to us as a gift. People sometimes go through days and weeks and years of absolute darkness, and then suddenly, perhaps coming from Communion, have such a sense of God that they have to go for a long walk. In the unutterable sweetness of that experience there is a great longing to be alone, and in that loneliness to know a companionship and a presence that is beyond all telling for beauty Christ came to be our way to the Father, to redeem us from our separation, that we might know, as He knew, what it is to be alone and yet not alone.

ADORATION AND THANKSGIVING

'I will praise the Name of God with a song, and will magnify Him with thanksgiving.'—Ps. lxix. 30

ADORATION and thanksgiving should be the chief part of our prayer. Our relationship to God when we come to pray is the relationship of those who adore Him because He is what He is. As we are filled with joy when we look upon some exquisite scene, so we adore God because of His transcendent and unutterable beauty. We adore Him because He has loved us, because He is Love ; because He has revealed Himself to us in a human life of unspeakable beauty and tenderness ; because when we treated Him worst, He treated us best ; because when we rejected Him, He did not reject us ; because His Holy Spirit is ever healing, restoring, and following us with mercy. We adore His unutterable love and His awful holiness.

Then we add to our worship thanksgiving. We thank Him for what He is in Himself, for what He is always doing. We thank Him for the self-giving which He has revealed in the Incarnation ; for His utter trust in the way of love, revealed by His death upon the Cross ; for the self-donation that goes on always in the mystery of the Blessed Sacrament. We thank Him for the love which is greater even than the sins of the world, the love which nothing can defeat and which must ultimately prevail. We thank Him that He has asked of us nothing but our love, and that, as we journey along the way He Himself has trodden, He not only leads us by His light but is Himself our companion. We thank Him that, being what He is and knowing what we are, He still loves us and longs to have us with Him for ever.

THE PRAYER OF REPARATION

'Overcome evil with good.'—ROM. xii. 21

ONE end of prayer is the end of satisfaction or reparation. If the Eternal Father was conscious in His supreme and infinite knowledge of anger, pride, and selfishness of all kinds in human nature, He was also conscious, when the Eternal Son became incarnate, of love, forgiveness, humility, unselfishness, and perfect beauty in that nature. The outrages hurled against the Creator, as human wills defied and insulted His majesty, were repaired by the perfection of obedience and beauty in the Sacred Humanity of His Son.

Even as our Lord Jesus Christ made one perfect, complete, and sufficient act of satisfaction for the sins of the whole world, so it is for the Church, which is the Body of Christ, and for every soul in the Church that makes up that Body, to be offering satisfaction and reparation ; against anger displaying forgiveness ; against self-indulgence, self-sacrifice ; against hate, love ; against doubt, faith ; against fear, courage. This relationship of satisfaction and reparation is a very precious part of prayer. It will be well for us if we let it take the place of criticism; if, when we hear of unbelief, we do not criticize the unbelief, but rather offer our own faith ; if, when we go to a church where the services are rendered in slovenly fashion, we do not talk about it but offer there our adoring worship, trying to give God our best where it seems to us He is receiving least ; offering Him satisfaction for sin, reparation for all the outrages and wounds of His love, and all that in union with the perfect satisfaction and reparation which is ever being offered to Him by the Sacred Humanity of His dear Son.

POINTS OF VIEW

'When the Comforter is come, Whom I will send unto you from the Father, even the Spirit of truth, which proceedeth from the Father, He shall testify of Me.'—S. JOHN xv. 26

WE want, as we think of the wonderful Ascension of our Lord, to remember the affectionate rebuke of the angel : ' Ye men of Galilee, why stand ye gazing up into heaven ? ' The august ritual with which our Lord ascended out of the sphere of sight and sound and touch was altogether appropriate to His passage hence, but all ritual is for the expression of reality, and the reality that this was meant to express was the giving to us of a great gift, that we, as the Collect says, may also ascend in heart and mind to where He has gone before. It is the supernatural point of view that we have to learn from this mystery.

The Holy Spirit is pledged to help us to see things from the point of view of Jesus. When in our life some bitter cup comes to us, we shall be able to see in that cup love's opportunity. If we yield ourselves in prayer to the Holy Spirit, things will begin to look quite different. As we see things from the supernatural point of view, we shall begin to meet them by supernatural methods. That is what conversion means. All our point of view is changed when we see in Jesus the love of God coming to save us, when we see in the Cross the wonderful revelation of that love going to the last length for our sakes, and when we think of ourselves as being the very children of God, loved by Him as Jesus was loved by Him, and taught to find in the various experiences of life the supernatural secret of spiritual ascension.

DISCIPLINE

'It is not for you to know the times or the seasons, which the Father hath put in His own power.'—Acts i. 7

THE last conversation which passed between our Lord and His disciples upon this earth, before He passed into the sphere of the Unseen, must have been an amazingly important conversation. Again and again the apostles must have turned back to it in their memories. There are three things which stand out in it. The first is disappointment, the second discipline, and the third a definite promise.

There is a story told of S. Teresa, that once, when she was praying, she got angry with God and thought He had treated her badly. She said, ' I do not wonder You have so few friends, when You treat them as You do !' If a great saint and contemplative felt that, we need not wonder if we sometimes feel God's ways are very strange. These apostles, who must surely have been going about with a thrilling expectation of wonders to come, are told just this—that it is not for them to know.

We too must expect discipline in our Christian life. This life of ours is for the making of saints. Every one of those men to whom our Lord was speaking was to go through some great trial, most of them to torture, almost all of them to martyrdom. If the first feeling is disappointment, the second must be a brave acceptance of discipline.

But there is this definite promise, that power will be given to witness to Christ, in whatever suffering or difficulty. Let us be content to go on bravely and prayerfully, to win the brave soul and the sure hope, more and more closely following Him Who passed by the way of the Manger and the Cross to the radiant glory of the day of the Ascension.

THE SACRED HUMANITY

'His dear Son . . . Who is the image of the invisible God.'
COL. i. 13, 15

THE Incarnation did not alter God, and so the life of Jesus our Lord is the eternal, self-sufficient, all-holy life of God, which the Son had for ever with the Father. Out of this rich life, in the counsels of God, came Jesus, the Divine Person, taking upon Him a human nature, and with that nature the power to die, the power to be tempted, and a human will that could choose in a human way. As we think of Jesus as wholly man, we have this amazing thing to consider—this Divine Person Who could not sin took to Himself a nature that could be tempted in every point as we are ; this Divine Person Who could not possibly die took to Himself a nature that could suffer the most terrible pain and the most awful death ; this Divine Person, wholly other to us, entered into this world of ours and functioned in this world in a human nature like our own.

Never until our Lord became incarnate did God see in human nature exactly what He wanted to see. We in our selves are something other than God meant us to be, but our Lord is exactly that which God meant Him to be. In Him we see this human nature of ours, free from all alliance with the smallest imperfection, completely expressing the divine idea which had called it into being.

In Christ our whole race is potentially redeemed. He has summed up all mankind in Himself, and ever presents to the Father a spotless humanity. What is true of Him may in our degree be true of us. In the Incarnation our Lord became present outside us ; by the grace of the Holy Spirit and the sacramental life He becomes, as it were, incarnate within us.

THE HOLY GHOST THE COMFORTER

*'I will pray the Father, and He shall give you another Comforter,
that He may abide with you for ever.'*—S. JOHN xiv. 16

GOD the Holy Trinity has had three great dealings with the
world : God the Father in creating it, God the Son in
redeeming it, God the Holy Spirit in bringing to fruition
the work of redemption.

We are living under the dispensation of God the Holy
Ghost. He is the power within us that fights against sin.
The yearning after God in prayer, all the soul's travail as it
searches after God, is His secret. Through Him we feel
contrition, and triumph over the temptation to despair.
Through His grace we make good confessions. It needs a
good deal of patience to be a true penitent. We get so tired
of falling. It often seems as if we were going back instead
of forward, as though it would have been much better if we
had never started. But the Holy Spirit gives the strength of
true penitence, which will not stay in that state of acquies-
cence with sin, and helps us to get up again, however many
times we fall.

We know how hard it is to witness for Christ. S. Peter
broke down before that test. It is not strange if we find it
very hard. Yet if we do witness to Him how happy we feel,
and that happiness is the joy of the Holy Ghost. The
supreme witness is that of the martyr. Often in life we are
faced with a choice. Shall we spare ourselves and live
quietly, keeping ourselves free of troubles and toil, or shall
we deliberately choose to do that which we know will in
the end wear us out and shorten our life ? Since the Holy
Ghost came at Pentecost the same power is with us that
enabled our Lord to set His face as a flint and go up to
Jerusalem.

THE HOLY GHOST THE ILLUMINATOR

'We all, with open face beholding as in a glass the glory of the Lord, are changed into the same image from glory to glory, even as by the Spirit of the Lord.'—2 COR. iii. 18

THE Holy Ghost is the interpreter of the Word of God. Many people saw Jesus, many people touched Him. Many saw Him heal the sick and do beautiful things, and many saw Him die. Only three saw Him transfigured, only some saw Him risen, only a few saw Him ascend into heaven. The power by which the apostles saw Jesus to be the Christ, the Son of the living God, was the power of the Holy Ghost. Only love can see the true beauty of the beloved. So Simeon and Anna, when He was a child, beheld Him. So the shepherds and Wise Men beheld His glory, as did the penitent thief, by the power of the Holy Ghost. Not to all men, or any particular class of men, was this power vouchsafed, but to any who had eyes to see and to whom the vocation was given.

The Holy Spirit illuminates the Church. The Church is composed of very human people, as the Bible is composed of very human stories. People can read the history of the Church without getting any profit, as they can read passages of the Bible to their hurt. None the less, the Church is the Body of Christ, and the Bible is the Word of God, and it is the Holy Spirit Who enables us to see this. The Church is the one kingdom which has an aristocracy of holiness, and holiness only, and the Bible is the one book that shows in all life the purposes of God and the education of conscience.

The Holy Ghost enables us to see the world as the world for which Christ died. Souls are always lovable, however much they sin. The Holy Spirit, Who pleads with souls, teaches us never to despair of souls.

FOUR FOUNDATIONS

According to the grace of God . . . as a wise master-builder, I have laid the foundation.'—1 Cor. iii. 10

There are four things necessary if worship is to be a reality. First, *a creed*—we cannot worship if we do not believe—and it must be a creed about a Divine Personality. One cannot worship a force or a tendency. It is a great matter to have a creed that we can say together, so that we can bring to our worship corporate faith.

Secondly, *a sacramental principle.* We cannot worship if we keep on earth the whole time. We must rise above ourselves, and yet we do not want to feel that the world is outside our sphere of worship. We want a meeting-place of what is here and what is above, a worship with a mystery in it, an interweaving of the seen and unseen, as we ourselves are soul and body.

Thirdly, *a sacrificial principle,* in order that we may become one with that which we offer. We want to unite ourselves with the Perfect Sacrifice.

Fourthly, we hunger for *a real communion with Him to Whom we make our offering.*

All this is fulfilled in the Blessed Eucharist. There we have creed, sacrament, sacrifice, and communion. We have to see to it that we take these four things out into our life. There must be a union between life and worship. If we are really living a life we believe in, that is creed in practice. If we are really building up the kingdom of heaven, life becomes sacramental. If we are really living for the kingdom at our own expense, that is sacrifice. If we are really living a life we can ask God to share, that is communion.

THE ULTIMATE AUTHORITY

'Prove all things ; hold fast that which is good.'—1 Thess. v. 21

THE problem of the future is really, ' What are men going to obey ? ' In the mediaeval world the authority of king and Pope was absolute, but that world has passed away, and we do not believe that any one would honestly wish it back again. What then is the ultimate authority, to which we can trust as to a sure guide, leading us more and more into all truth ? For each soul this must be the ultimate authority of his own spiritual experience.

The Church's treasure is the spiritual experience of her saints, and it is to this really that the Church points as her claim to hold the truth that is the solution of the world's needs. The plenary inspiration of the Bible, the scientific interpretation of life, individual declarations of doctrine from the greatest theologians, all these would not help unless they tallied with the fundamental experience of the human soul. Christ Himself is the interpreter of experience, and experience finds its interpretation in Christ. As the Church seeks, interprets, and nourishes spiritual experience, so she leads her children to the ultimate union for which we pray.

S. Paul spoke of his own individual life as God's revelation of His Son in him. ' When it was the good pleasure of God to reveal His Son in me,' he writes, ' immediately I conferred not with flesh and blood . . . I went to Arabia ' (*Gal.* i). Out of his spiritual experience came his submission to the Catholic Church. A sane submission to the Church is just the attitude of humility in the presence of great spiritual experience, and the glad contribution of one's own to the welcoming experience of the rest.

A DOOR, A RAINBOW, A THRONE

'Behold, a door was opened in heaven . . . and a throne was set in heaven . . . and there was a rainbow round about the throne.'

REV. iv. 1-3

THESE three things are brought before us, a door, a rainbow, and a throne, and they may stand for the three great theological virtues and the three Persons of the Trinity.

The door may stand to us for faith. It may also stand for the Incarnation of the Son of God. It is through the door of the Incarnation that the great God entered into the heart of humanity. We could never have known God as we Christians know Him, if He had not found that door into our hearts, and given us that door into *His* heart, the door which is itself a Heart, the Sacred Heart of Jesus. The door may stand to us for that great virtue of faith, without which life would have no peace and no beauty ; also for the wonderful mystery in which Jesus came from the heart of the Father to our heart.

Round the throne, we are told, there was a rainbow, and a rainbow always stands for hope, hope shining through the darkness and the storm. There is not only a rainbow round the throne but about the world, and that is the assurance that behind all things there is a will and a mind shaping things to a purpose. The rainbow stands for the Holy Spirit Who is shaping the world, Who shaped the body which Jesus wore.

Then there was a throne, and on the throne a Presence, the regnant presence of the God Who is Love. Life is not really life unless there is love, and it is absolutely necessary that the Transcendent God should have in Himself the relationships which make love possible. God is a Trinity because He is Love, and also a Unity because He is Love ; in the one Love there are three Persons.

TRINITY IN UNITY

'The fair beauty of the Lord.'—Ps. xxvii. 4

WE constantly find that things go in threes. It is only a trinity very often that can make a perfect unity. Holiness, Beauty, and Truth represent such a trio. The Catholic Church that we must live and work for, must hold within itself these three in a right proportion. As we look on life within the Church and beyond its pale, we shall constantly find one of the three missing.

As we study the history of the Church, we always find in her buildings and her services, her teaching and the lives of her saints, the note of holiness and beauty, and there has always been much devotion to what is called ' the Truth.' But let a Galileo scientifically set out on the quest for truth, and he will do it at the risk of his life.

The first Puritans had a forbidding sort of holiness, and some of them had a great regard for truth, but what about beauty ? The empty niches, the ancient glass and beautiful buildings that they destroyed, all cry out against them.

The world of art has made a quest of beauty, and has also paid homage to truth, but poets and artists, writers and musicians, actors and actresses, have not been pre-eminently renowned for their holiness.

This ought not to be, for we feel instinctively—that is, most surely and truly—that Beauty is not true unless it is holy, that Holiness is not true unless it is beautiful, and that the Truth must also be both beautiful and holy. The fight of the future will be to set these three graces on their pedestal together, for God is the absolute Truth, the supreme Holiness, and the ultimate and adorable Beauty.

74

HE FIRST

'We love Him, because He first loved us.'—1 S. JOHN iv. 19

THERE are some truths which make the whole difference to life, and the thought of the priority of God is one of them. God is first in priority of time. In the story of Genesis (and science tells us the same thing) the world was got ready for man before man came into it. Beauty was fashioned before the eye was fashioned to see it. The songs of the birds, the sigh of the wind, and the sound of the sea, were all there before the ear. We live because God first lived. The world of speculation that scientific people give us only puts the mystery a little further back. They never can tell us of the First Cause. There is no other answer but that which our faith gives us, that God is first. The supreme peace, the supreme answer to our minds, is in that knowledge. All is really well with the world if God created it, if God is behind it. Whatever hands we may fall into, we can never fall out of the hands of God. When we approach the last experience of death, we shall be passing through an experience that is just as much in the control of God as was our birth.

Our second thought is of the priority of God's love. As God ever lived, so God ever loved. He loved us before we had any thought of loving Him. It is so in natural love. When a baby is born, the mother loves the baby because it is her own child, not because it is a good baby or because it loves her. God loves us because we are His children. If we live because He first lived, we also love because He first loved.

GOD OUR HELPER

'My help cometh from the Lord.'—Ps. cxxi. 2

If God is first in priority of time, if God is first in the priority of love, it follows that God must have a priority in my life and yours, that He must have a priority in every choice of ours, and we must frame our lives on this standard—' Is this thing that I am going to do, is this thing that I am going to say, is this idea that I am going to frame and carry out, something that I can lay before God and ask His blessing upon ?' That will give us a great confidence and a great peace. It does not matter how hard the day's work is if we can say, 'This is what my Father wants me to do, and I know perfectly well that He will help me to do it.'

Let us try very simply and humbly to render our lives to God and make Him first in our lives. In a sense there is no such thing as time. What we call time is just a moment of eternity, and we can bring heaven into our lives here if we will. If some great friendship or joy has come into our life, let us think that God was there first ; that love is ours because God loved first ; that joy is to be turned into thanksgiving. If we have some great sorrow, some bitter pain, God is there first, God knows all about it. He is watching and waiting to see that this last tragedy shall not happen—that we should be defeated by our sorrow and gain no spiritual education from its experience. God, Who has worn a crown of thorns, knows all about our sorrow and can enter into it and make it beautiful.

DIVES AND LAZARUS

'He that dwelleth in love dwelleth in God, and God in him. Herein is our love made perfect, that we may have boldness in the day of judgement.'—1 S. JOHN iv. 16, 17

THE great broad principles that this parable sets forth are : that there is a life after this life, and our condition in that life is affected by our behaviour in this ; that there are what may be represented as great gulfs, that is to say, terminations to times of opportunity ; that if people cannot hear the call of duty, they will not hear the call of miracles. The parable gives us two types, a Job type that is not defeated by pain and poverty, and an Ahab type that is defeated by position and riches.

1. The first thought is the preciousness of our own souls. We do not want to pose as publicans, and thank God we are not Pharisees. We shall not be at all like Lazarus, if we thank God we are not Dives ! But we have patiently to return again and again to this great truth, that it is the soul that matters. We want good conditions for people that their souls may have a better chance, but our faith as Christians is that souls can rise above circumstances.

2. There do come limits of opportunity. If we have wronged some one let us make it up before the gulf of death divides us. Here on earth we have the royal prerogative of living by faith. We cannot see the shining walls of the city, the bridal beauty of the Church, the Spouse of Christ, but we have the honour of walking by faith. Let us use that opportunity before it vanishes in sight.

3. We believe in a sacramental religion, not a sensational religion. The truth would not be more true if it were proclaimed by a visitant from another world. There is only one Truth, and that is for all time because it is above all time.

A SACRAMENTAL SENSE

'God hath said, I will dwell in them, and walk in them ; and I will be their God, and they shall be My people.'—2 COR. vi. 16

THAT verse may be our text as we try to think of a sacramental sense. A sacramental sense is the recognition that one's body, the world of nature, and everything made by God was meant for His possession and self-expression. When we find God in the Blessed Sacrament, we begin to find sacrament in all things. Labour, if we look at it sacramentally, becomes service, and its priest is the Carpenter of Nazareth. Art becomes worship, and its priest is the Lord of the lilies and the rainbow. Science becomes the quest of God's creative purposes, and its priest is the Word of God. All is captured, and all is made radiant and splendid. Even the greatest pain and the greatest agony may be consecrated to become the soul's best sacrifice, and the consecrating priest will be the Lord of Calvary. We can find in suffering and sorrow the Real Presence of the Man of Sorrows.

The Blessed Sacrament shines before us as the very goal and apex of creation, the thing created by, wholly possessed by, and wholly expressive of, the Creator. We, His children, feed upon that mystery and are made one with His life, and all the actions of our life should become sacramental. Our hands should become healing and creative hands, our lips should speak Gospel messages—all that our hearts, our hands, our minds, our whole being can do should become expressive of that Life which is becoming our own life. So gradually the kingdoms of this world shall become the kingdom of God, the children of men shall become the children of God, life shall become worship, and death shall be life's last sacrifice of love.

THE SACRED HEART

'Now, O Lord, Thou art our father.'—Isa. lxiv. 8

THAT which makes home heaven is that which makes heaven home, and that is the reign there of a true and tender heart. When we speak of home, we do not mean bricks and mortar : when we speak of heaven, we do not really mean streets of gold and crystal seas, still less having everything we want. We cannot rest in that kind of thing. We cannot doubt that any world that is wholly God's creation is altogether lovely and beautiful, but when we think about heaven as our home it is not because heaven is beautiful, but because God is there and we find our abiding-place in His Heart. As has been admirably said by a good Frenchman, ' We do not find God in heaven, but we find heaven in God.' That is because we find home in God. The Sacred Heart is our sure home, and we must return again and again to that home in our prayer.

The Sacred Heart is a faithful heart. Probably we have all been faithful to some people but unfaithful to others. We have ' let them down,' as we say. The Heart of Jesus has never let any one down. Our hope for the world, for the Church, for the great body of Christian people outside the Church, for our own solitary soul, is in His faithfulness. The apostles had their differences, S. Paul sometimes withstood S. Peter to the face, but their union was in the Heart of Jesus. It is the same with us to-day. There are many divisions amongst Christian people, but when we are troubled about the divisions in the Church, we can remember that there is one Heart which is always faithful, and if we are tempted to despair of union amongst ourselves we may none the less have hope of union in Him.

INTEGRITY

'Thou shalt go before the face of the Lord to prepare His ways.'
S. LUKE i. 76

S. JOHN the Baptist stands out pre-eminent for the complete integrity of his character. He was ready to decrease in order that Christ might increase, to sacrifice himself wholly for the cause. Many people are ready to fight for a good cause, provided they themselves are in the front rank, but when for the good of the cause it would be better for them to give place to another, they go out of the battle altogether. S. John was completely ready to take a lower place, and to see his own disciples leave him and follow Jesus. Again, he was ready to say the same thing in any company. He preached the same doctrine in the royal chapel as in the market-place, and, if he taught the publicans that they must give up their sins, he also denounced the crime of Herod, who was living with his brother's wife. He gave our Lord that purest devotion, that he was ready to leave Jesus for Jesus' sake, to go from the manifest presence in the home of Nazareth to labour in the wilderness for the coming of the kingdom.

It is part of the training of our character that we should recognize that there is much we cannot do ; all we can do is to make ourselves instruments in God's hands, to use or lay aside. Our part may be to sow that others may reap, and we must be ready to stand aside for the good of the cause. We must try to get that integrity of character which will make us perfect servants in the cause of the kingdom. There is often a vocation to follow S. John the Baptist in leaving conditions where we have spiritual luxury, to labour in self-effacing ways that in some wilderness the Faith may be born.

THE EDUCATION OF A SAINT

'Learn to do well.'—Isa. i. 17

It is a great thing to consider that a saint can make mistakes and can learn from them. S. Peter made mistakes, but he learnt by making them. He was mistaken in three things : in his thoughts about our Lord, about the saints, and about himself. He was mistaken in his thought about Christ. He could believe in a Christ, and he could believe that Jesus was the Christ, but he could not believe in a crucified Christ. When our Lord spoke to His disciples of what was coming upon Him, S. Peter rebuked Him and said, ' That be far from Thee, Lord.' He had to learn the wonder of the Holy Cross—and he did learn.

Again, he was mistaken about the saints. On the Mount of Transfiguration, when the three apostles beheld Moses and Elias with our Lord, he exclaimed, ' Let us make three tabernacles : one for Thee, and one for Moses, and one for Elias.' He thought he could capture saints upon a mountain and find heaven in a place. He had to learn that he could only have Moses and Elias with him as he gained the character of Moses and Elias, and gained true communion of soul with those heaven-taught spirits. He had to learn that only could he abide with Jesus as he learned the mind of Jesus.

Then he was mistaken about himself. He thought he could be faithful though others were faithless, that though others might flee he would not, and he had to learn by his own fall true humility and the lesson of complete dependence upon his Master. He had to learn to say, as S. Paul said : ' O wretched man that I am ! Who shall deliver me from the body of this death ? I thank God through Jesus Christ our Lord.'

THE ROCK MAN

'Thou art Peter, and upon this rock I will build My Church'
S. MATT. xvi. 18

As our Lord built the house of His life upon the foundation of faith in the Divine Love, so He could only build the house of His Church on the foundation of faith in Himself. When Peter by the inspiration of the Holy Ghost cried, ' Thou art the Christ, the Son of the living God,' our Lord felt that He had found the rock faith on which He could begin to build.

If we consider the three typical names by which our Lord called His apostle—Simon, Peter, and Satan—Simon may stand for the natural man, Peter for the redeemed man, and Satan for the rebellious man. All of us are in our first natural beginning Simon, born into this world with natural desires and the power of choice. But right at our birth the Church of Christ meets us and puts us into the supernatural order by baptism ; and as our minds develop and our wills become more definitely our own, there is presented to us more and more clearly the Gospel and the Person of Christ, that we may make our personal choice. All of us who have felt the spell of His beauty have cried out at some time, ' Thou art the Christ ! ' and so passed from the state of Simon to the state of Peter. Each one of us has to make that confession of faith. But when we have made that personal acceptance of our Lord, then we have to learn the lesson of the Cross, and to accept Him as the crucified, suffering Messiah, taking up our cross for His sake, that we may not fall into condemnation and merit the rebuke of the name of Satan, the Adversary

IDEAS AND CONVICTIONS: I

'*Now all the Athenians and the strangers sojourning there spent their time in nothing else, but either to tell or to hear some new thing.*'

ACTS xvii. 21, R.V.

To the city of Athens, which abounded with ideas, came one man with a few convictions. It is not a bad thing to have ideas which are the fruit of convictions, nor is it a bad thing to begin with ideas that shape and solidify until they become convictions ; but one cannot live on ideas, still less can one die for them or in the strength of them. If one is to live, rather than exist, and to live effectively, one must have convictions. People have ideas about God, religion, the Church, a future life. Ideas are many, convictions few.

Saul of Tarsus once had wrong convictions, and that made him a power for evil. He believed that ' God so loved ' the Jews that any one who seemed to rival Moses must be treated as an enemy, so he could stand and watch Stephen being stoned to death and approve of it. Now he came to a Greek multitude that was flirting with many ideas, with a strong and true conviction that Christ is the one answer to every need. So he came to be a power for good.

All great doctrine has really proceeded from the conviction of experience, and has only been expressed in order to be the protection of that experience. The Church's experience came before the Church's creed. In her creed she has expressed her convictions in order to protect her children from the ephemeral ideas of men.

IDEAS AND CONVICTIONS: II

*'Be ye also ready : for in such an hour as ye think not the Son of Man
cometh.'*—S. MATT. xxiv. 44

OUR Lord stood at the parting of the ways. He saw that
disasters were coming upon His own nation, He spoke of
strife and pestilence and famine, of awesome signs and
fearful sights, of men's hearts failing them for fear because
all their ideas of heaven and earth and security would be
shaken. But He bid them rest in the great conviction that
these were not the throes of death but the pangs of travail.
He bade them possess their souls in patience, that through
the very sufferings of that time they might be born again
to a new knowledge of God and a new vision of the kingdom,
as He Himself through the travail of the Passion was to pass
to the glory of the Resurrection life.

Probably all the industrial troubles of our day are due to
the fact that the religion of most men consists of ideas rather
than convictions. As Christians, we ought to have three
great convictions : that God is our Father, and that we are
all made in His image ; that He has been revealed to us in
Christ ; that we are all brethren, and that so mankind is one
great family. If they were convictions, they would not be
shaken. It is because for most of us they are only ideas that
we fail to claim the whole world and every department of life
for Christ. When our faith indeed becomes conviction, it
can change not only the individual but the whole world.

LOST AND FOUND

'Until he find it.'—S. LUKE xv. 4

In this Gospel we have stories of three lost things : a lost piece of silver, a lost sheep, and a lost son. They stand for three different kinds of ' lostness.'

The piece of silver has no responsibility for the fact that it is lost. In the great tender mind of our Almighty Father, as revealed by our Lord in these stories, it seems that there are souls whose lostness is almost no responsibility of their own. This story gives us God's judgement on bad environment and the way to deal with it. There is no blame attached to the coin, but the woman (who may stand for the Church) has to get the environment right. She must light the house and clean it, and then she will have a chance of finding the coin.

There is not a great deal of responsibility to be attached to the sheep ; it has wandered away through silliness. This is the great parable of missionary work and adventure. We have to go to any place where the sheep is, however dangerous, and save the sheep there.

The lost son has been taught and is a responsible person, and the good father does not go out after him   He leaves him alone. The son has a free will, and must be allowed to go to the far country and spend his money as he likes. When he realizes the folly of his choice and accepts his responsibility for that folly in an act of penitence, his act of penitence is not more swift than the coming of the father's love, meeting him on his way, to restore him to his true place in his own home.

LIGHTEN OUR DARKNESS

'He that doeth the truth cometh to the light.'—S. JOHN iii. 21, R.V.

WHEN our Lord spoke about there being so many hours in the day in which a man might walk and work, and then of the night coming which brought the opportunity to an end, He was emphasizing that we have in ourselves no sufficiency of light to walk and work by. We depend upon the light which is given to us, and without this given light from the sun or the candle we must stumble. That which is true naturally is true spiritually. We have not light in ourselves ; we need the supernatural Light which He is and which He gives us.

Though we have no light in ourselves, we have an organ which can correspond to the light, our eye. If our eye is normal and in health, it rejoices in the light ; but if it is affected in some way, we cannot stand the light and want to get away from it. The same is true spiritually. With the life that was given to us was also given the power to apprehend the light of the Life that brought us into being. This organ of our souls we call our conscience. If there is something wrong with our conscience, we are afraid of Him and would hide away from His light. But if our conscience is healthy, then we rejoice in the light of the Lord, and gladly follow Him and accept the education which He gives us, learning more and more to rejoice in the sureness of His leading and our own sense of being rightly led. Just as we expect the sun to shine and walk confidently in its light, so we learn to expect His light to shine upon us, and walk confidently in the light which comes to us from Him through His Spirit.

THE RISE OF MAN

'As we have borne the image of the earthy, we shall also bear the image of the heavenly.'—I Cor. xv. 49

As science has sought and nature has yielded up her treasures, and the earth has whispered the secrets of God hidden in the mystery of her creation, it seems that the scheme of God's fashioning was something like this. After the prologue in the spirit-world, which is dimly revealed to us in the story of the angels and their fall, God created matter. Everything God called into being He made for enrichment, and so to matter He added life ; to life He added instinct, and later reason ; and when this organic evolution was finished, man was given the power of exercising his free will, and in the wrong use of this power came his fall.

Then in the fullness of time came Christ our Lord, to satisfy by His gift of grace that spiritual longing implanted in our nature by God, and educated by the prophetic ministry and the teaching of the Holy Spirit. Even as in organic evolution there has been an ascension from matter to man-hood, however that came about, so there became possible a spiritual evolution which should lift manhood to Christhood, and which, if there had been no sin, might have gone forward without travail or tragedy. In this spiritual evolution we can take our deliberate part, or we can, if we will, go back to the ways of the barbarian and the ape. We do not know, and there is no great need that we should, how far in detail the hypothesis of evolution is true. There can be little doubt that in some degree it is true. We can be sure of this, that even as the Gospel is true, so all truth is really gospel, and we can set against the sad experience of a fall the good news of man's potential rise.

WHAT IS SIN?

'Against Thee only have I sinned.'—Ps. li. 4

WHAT is sin? Sin is the association of one's will with something which is contrary to the will of the Divine Love. There must be behind this universe and all the laws that govern it one supreme all-holy Will. If I set my will in defiance to that Will, there must be discord. I am a sinner, and I am sinning against Him. God is Love, and all His laws are based on love, all His desires are desires of love. The sinful thought, the sinful act, the sinful word, is really always an unloving thought, an unloving act, an unloving word. The sinful act is always an act of selfishness.

Sin to the Pharisee was doing or not doing a definite act. The Pharisees had a clear list of acts which were sinful, of acts which were not sinful, and of obligations which a devout Jew had to fulfil. There it began and there it ended. Sin to our Lord was the thing that separated the child of God from God, and that is never just an act but a spiritual condition behind an act. Two acts might be the same, but might have altogether different spiritual qualities behind them. The Pharisee in the parable had behind his outward piety an inward condition of pride and self-satisfaction : the Publican had behind his outward sense of sin and self-abasement a hunger for God which made him more the child of God than the Pharisee. All through the history of the Church the temptation has been to concentrate not upon a spiritual condition but upon certain acts. It is so much easier. Yet it was always interior integrity that our Lord taught, and always the loss of that which had for Him the quality of sin.

SPIRITUAL CONDITION

'Every one that is perfect shall be as his master.'—S. LUKE vi. 40

To our Lord that was sin which separated the soul from God, and that was right which brought about the union of the soul with God. When the woman taken in adultery was brought by her accusers and cast down before our Lord, they said, 'This woman has done a sinful act. Moses commanded that people who committed that act should be stoned. What do you say?' Our Lord lifted it all into the atmosphere of spiritual condition. He said, 'If there is any man whose spiritual condition makes him fit to cast a stone at that woman, let that man cast the first stone.' Then He bowed His head and wrote in the sand, and when He lifted His head again every one of her accusers had passed out. They knew that, though they might not have committed the sin the woman had committed, their spiritual condition did not justify them in condemning her in the presence of our Lord.

We see how wonderful, how very difficult, our religion is. Purity according to the Pharisees consisted in certain acts of purification. To our Lord purity was a spiritual state, a very much harder thing to attain. It takes ever so much more trouble to get alone with our Father and pray things out. The woman's act was the symptom of a condition. It was the condition that Christ cared about. A good doctor does not concentrate upon a symptom : he concentrates upon the condition of which the symptom is a revelation. Sin is not just this or that act. It is a spiritual condition of separation from love, from spiritual beauty, which has resulted, and must inevitably result, in this or that act of unloveliness.

CONFIDENCE IN GOD

'Though He slay me, yet will I trust in Him.'—JOB xiii. 15

FAITH is an infused grace of God. This does not mean that God gives us the power to believe things that are very difficult to believe intellectually. The gift of faith goes deeper than the intellect. It is really the spiritual power of confidence in God, which enables the soul to go on in spite of the difficulties of life.

It seems to be God's way first to give this confidence in Him to the soul, and then to leave the life to be, as it might seem, the sport of circumstances, the soul all the while being sustained by God's gift of interior confidence, the character being formed and perfected by exterior blows and buffetings and apparently complete neglect. It often appears to any one who only looks on the surface of things as if God abandons most the souls that have abandoned themselves to Him, as if He treats worst those who love Him best.

The key to this mystery is the Cross of our Lord Jesus Christ. God wants witnesses in this world, and the best witness to His love and beauty is the great Cross of Christ and the lesser crosses of His saints. It would be a very elementary Christian who could imagine that being a Christian meant having a good time Being a Christian means following Christ, and our Lord never offered a good time to anybody. He said, ' If any man will come after Me, let him deny himself and take up his cross and follow Me,' and the power that enables a soul to take up its cross and follow Christ and go on following Him is this deep interior confidence in God.

THE GENEROSITY OF GOD : I

'God loveth a cheerful giver.'—2 Cor. ix. 7

WHAT God loves in others He is in Himself, and we can take this charming trait in the Divine Nature, this cheerful giving or generosity, and see how every article of our faith proceeds quite naturally from this fundamental virtue in the character of the good God.

We believe in the Blessed Trinity. We could not believe in a unit God, who was ever in the condition of having no one to love ; one whose existence could not really be life, because having great riches there was no one to share them with. If God the Creator, transcendent above all things and prior to all things, and without relationship outside Himself, had not had relationships within Himself, it is very difficult to see how He could ever have become conscious of His own existence. It is hardly possible to be Love and to have no one and nothing to love, and certainly such a state is not thinkable of a perfect Being.

The unity of God is not numerical but essential, and that essential unity is interpreted in the perfect generosity of the three Divine Persons of the Sacred Trinity in their ideal mutual love for each other. In one of our creeds we assert confidently that ' in this Trinity none is afore, or after other : none is greater, or less than another ; but the whole three Persons are co-eternal together : and co-equal.' That is to say, we believe that no words can sufficiently express the utter generosity and self-giving of the love of the three Divine Persons for one another : they are only at the best a human makeshift for expressing what no human language can express, the perfect generosity of the character of God in His own essential being.

THE GENEROSITY OF GOD : II

'God so loved the world, that He gave His only begotten Son.'
S. JOHN iii. 16

THE Incarnation reveals to us that generosity in giving which is part of the adorable character of God. Coming to His world and making Himself known to it, He willed to come in the most generous way possible, in the way which would be the greatest help and blessing to those who most needed help and blessing. He came to lay His head in the place of poverty, He willed that His cradle should be the poorest of all cradles and His quilt the cheapest of all quilts, and He lay there in the generosity of His self-oblation with the wood of the manger beneath Him and the straw of the stable about Him, the great God manifest under the guise of the poorest little Baby that ever was born.

All through His life He was consistent. He saved for Himself no privileges. He did not go off to heaven for week-ends ! He, Who made all things, made chairs and tables, and yokes for oxen, and oars for boats, and the simple things the village needed ; in the utter generosity of His love sharing truly and really, without the slightest bit of unreality in it, the actual life of a working man of that age and generation.

In His death His generosity reached its climax. There we see Him not passing from the Mount of Transfiguration through an adoring company of angels to that glory which was His by essential right, but making His death for us the way of life, and bringing comfort and comradeship to two wrecked lives as He hung on the mount of shame betwixt the thieves ; and as He passed from His Passion to paradise, it was a thief whom He took for His companion as He made His human entry into the world of spirits.

92

THE GENEROSITY OF GOD : III

'Who gave Himself for our sins, that He might deliver us.'—GAL. i. 4.

WE see God's generosity revealed to us in the Sacraments of His Church. We say in our creed that we believe in ' the forgiveness of sins,' and indeed we ought to, if we think of the parables in which our Lord speaks of forgiveness. There is the story He tells of the unmerciful servant : this man owed an immense sum and asked for time to pay it ; the lord in the parable gave him more than he asked, he forgave him the whole debt. In the parable the generosity of God is contrasted with the lack of generosity in men. The story was told for the benefit of S. Peter and the apostles, who had thought that seven times was a very generous number with which to count one's forgiveness of the same person, and was an illustration of what our Lord meant by ' seventy times seven.'

We have to remember, though, that the generosity of God cuts both ways. It cuts the bonds of those who come to Him for mercy : it cuts off from Him those who are not themselves generous to their brethren. We can, if we will, refuse to enter into the joy of our Lord.

Again, in the greatest Sacrament of all, one reason why we believe so passionately in the reality of the Gift that is given to us, that it is indeed Jesus Himself, the Bread of Heaven, Whom we receive in our Communion, is because such a self-giving is alone consistent with the generosity of God.

THE SENSE OF VOCATION

'At Thy word I will.'—S. LUKE v. 5

WHEN our Lord said to S. Peter, ' Launch out into the deep, and let down your nets,' and the apostle answered, ' At Thy word I will,' he was not going to do something different to what he had been doing daily, but this very commonplace thing he had been constantly doing he did now with a sense of vocation and as an act of responsive obedience. The sense of vocation may alter the whole condition of a life. It may take a man from an office to the priesthood, as it took Matthew from his customs to his discipleship. It may take a priest into the religious life or out to the mission-field. But it may, on the other hand, only change the motive and quality of the life, leaving it the same, but transfigured and vastly enriched, as it is lifted from a profession to a vocation.

All English law is based on the axiom that we are responsible people. We are responsible for our acts, and indeed also for our thoughts. We are conscious of a world of spirit, of which the hidden laws are the principles of good and evil. Our sense of moral responsibility makes us discriminate between them, and our sense of vocation is the realization that the good are projections of the mind of a Lawgiver Who is personally interested in us and has revealed Himself personally in Christ. As the scientific mind brings itself to bear upon natural laws in a scientific way, so the spiritual mind brings its allegiance to spiritual laws in a vocational way, in the deliberate following of a God Who with the voice of Christ is ever calling the soul to a higher holiness.

THE WAY OF APPEAL

'Where the Spirit of the Lord is, there is liberty.'—2 Cor. iii. 17

Our Lord had one reason for doing all He did, and that was because it was the Father's will. But that will of His Father was a moral height and spiritual splendour to which His own soul rose with an entire acceptance and embrace. It was never the imposing of a will that crushed His own will, but the attraction of a will that was utterly holy. If we let a human will dominate our will, it is very bad for our will. But if we let the Will of God dominate our will, it will set us free. God's service is the only service which is perfect freedom. There are no terrors in God's call, no risks in trusting Him. There are no regrets in the surrender of the will to God.

God's way is always the way of appeal, and we may well meditate on His wisdom in this. If we dictate to people, we draw out of them what is bad. We get from them either subservience or subterfuge or rebellion. But if we appeal to people, we draw out of them what is good. The little hands held out to us from the straw-filled bed at Bethlehem, the blessed hands spread abroad on the Cross, the whispered words, ' Do this in remembrance of Me,' make an amazing appeal. God's vocation is an appeal, the appeal of holiness, the appeal of innocence, the appeal of suffering, the appeal of the memory of a friend, and it is all a call to be. Even as our Lord in His self-revealing is God's appeal to us, in His human obedience He is the revelation of the perfection that must follow a surrender to the appeal of the everlasting holiness and love of the Blessed Trinity.

THE COMMON SENSE OF PRAYER

' Pray without ceasing.'—I THESS. v. 17

THE true solution of all our troubles is in the way of prayer. ' Ask, and ye shall receive,' says our Lord ; ' knock, and it shall be opened unto you.' That is common sense. If we want to get into a house, we do not walk about outside ; we go to the door and knock. ' Seek, and ye shall find.' If we want to find something, we do not moon about with our heads in the air ; we get a light and go down on our knees and look for it. ' Lay up for yourselves treasure in heaven.' We must put money into the bank before we can draw out.

People sometimes say they find it hard to come into retreat, even from Friday to Monday, because they have so much to do. Our Lord had much more to do. He had not to alter a home, a business, or a parish, but to alter a world ! He had only three years to do it in, and He started with forty days in retreat

Even when He had worked all day, He prayed all night. The supreme thing in His life was prayer. It was through prayer that He learnt to turn suffering into obedience and to see in every event of life, as it came to Him, an opportunity of behaving in those circumstances, whatever might be their human cause, with the divine love which would make His conduct the revelation of the Word of God.

THE QUEEN OF PENITENTS

'The devil said unto Him, All this power will I give Thee.'
S. LUKE iv. 6

To all of us sooner or later comes a consciousness of power
of some sort. Mary Magdalene realized the power of her
womanhood and used it for evil ends, earning for herself
the title of ' Mary of the seven devils,' seven being a full
number. When she saw the humble carpenter of Nazareth
pass down the street, it was probably with the kind of feeling
that a woman of her type might have, that her power was
being challenged by a purity that stood above it. So she drew
near to Him, to meet the look of One Who felt for her
womanhood only reverence, pity, hope, and love.

As she met the look of Jesus, she saw what her life had
missed, what her life might have been if she had met Him
before she sinned. But He Who looked on her gave to her
the revelation of the Lord and Lover of her soul, and her soul
rose from its charnel-house to greet the Lord of its life, as
Lazarus rose from his tomb. She rose out of her old life
which was really death, to follow Him to that death which
was the perfect fulfilment of life, the perfect sacrifice of love.
She became the companion of Christ and the men who were
with Him, and her womanhood was turned into a healing
power, and even her experience of evil was brought to the
treasury of Christ's Church. She became for all time the
queen of penitents, and no poor girl can ever be without hope,
as she turns her thoughts to Mary Magdalene, who rose
from the depths to which her seven devils drew her to share
with Mary the Mother her vigil by the Cross.

SACRAMENTAL ACTS

*'Except your righteousness shall exceed the righteousness of the Scribes
and Pharisees, ye shall in no case enter into the kingdom of heaven.'*
S. MATT. v. 20

ALL our acts are in a sense sacramental acts : they are
expressive of some kind of real presence. A simple act may
have in it the real presence of a great vocation, and a small
act may have in it the real presence of a great hatred. Man's
acts of sin are, so to speak, sacramentally evil—outward and
visible signs of a vitiated sinful will, a means whereby that
will is made manifest even to the moderate intelligence of
man, and more surely to the unerring wisdom of God. Our
Lord has told us what sin there may be in a look, and yet
our eyes are perfectly innocent things. But the outward is
effectually expressive of the inward ; if the inward is evil,
then our acts and words are the expression of an essential
evil ; and if the inward is pure and right, acts and words are
the veils of the reality of a pure intention. Our words and
acts are always outward and visible signs of the inward
intention. Sin and virtue in their essence are not in the act,
but in the will behind the act.

Man's repentance is the dissociation of his will from the
thoughts, words, and deeds that have been the expression of
some evil intention, and the association of his will with
thoughts, words, and deeds which are expressive of real
contrition, and so man makes his repentance sacramentally.
Man's highest glory is when he deliberately associates his
will with acts of sacrifice. There he attains most nearly to
the absolute liberty of God. Such acts need not necessarily
be acts of suffering, though acts of suffering are sure to be
amongst such acts, but they will be acts of pure worship and
pure unselfishness, the sacramental expression of a holy will.

THE KING AND THE BEGGAR-MAID

'The Lord hath appeared of old unto me, saying, . . . I have loved thee with an everlasting love.'—JER. xxxi. 3

THE story of Cinderella, who sat among the ashes and wedded the king's son, and the tale of King Cophetua and the beggar-maid, have always held our imagination, perhaps because, unconsciously to ourselves, they are parables of a great spiritual truth. Each one of us is so dear, so precious to God, that we may quite truly think of our soul as the spouse of the Holy Ghost, the beggar-maid whom the King loves.

This should make us, first of all, very humble people, as we think of the great King Who has loved so ardently our shabby little souls, we so careless and He caring so much. We look up at Jesus on the Cross, and see in Him the revelation of God's care for us. That was the price that He thought it worth while paying for these cheap souls of ours.

So our humility turns to pride, and we become very proud people. We may be quite alone because we are trying to serve God, we may be crushed because we are trying to be true to His principles, but we have a happy secret, because we are so proud of His love. Martyrs have felt that the physical pain mattered nothing in comparison with the secret communion with their Lord that their witness of suffering won for them. We may be proud that, though our souls may seem so shabby in our own sight, and the sight of the rest of the world, in His sight we are so precious.

ABLE

'Are ye able?' *'We are able.'* *'Ye shall.'*

S. MATT. xx. 22, 23

THESE two great saints of God, James and his brother John, were human, and had their weaknesses, but they had also their splendour. When they were asked if they were able to drink of this cup and be baptized with this baptism, there was something magnificent in their answer, ' We are able.' Our Lord, looking at them with love, and perhaps ineffable sadness, said, ' Ye shall.' As they stood by His side in the splendour of their young manhood they little dreamed of the things that life would bring them. They had to see Jesus dying on the Cross ; there came a day when James was thrown into prison and knew that on the morrow the sword of the executioner would fall on him ; John had to live through years of exile. But we know how in those two splendid men it was fulfilled that they were able to drink of the cup their Lord drank of and glorify God.

There is a time when our religion seems a completely thrilling thing, that no power could ever defeat. That is what James and John had known. But the same Lord Who has opened to us the splendour and reality of spiritual things, will surely ask us one day if we can drink a cup and bear a baptism which will be for us our own particular share in His Passion. That day, when it comes, will be the supreme opportunity of our religion and will bring its own grace with it. We shall be able to drink of that cup, and give Him glory in the day of trial.

THOSE THINGS AND THESE THINGS

'The end of those things is death.'—ROM. vi. 21

THE whole of the Epistle of S. Paul to the Romans is the setting forth of a contrast between two states of life. S. Paul is putting before his spiritual children the different ends of life. 'Those things' are what he calls 'life after the flesh,' that is, the natural life apart from Christ. 'These things' are what Christ Himself called 'the life more abundant,' that is, human life lived in union with Him.

There is no romance about a sinful life. One sinner behaves like another, and always has. We live in a world which is based on moral laws and on the law of human responsibility. Our actions have certain and scientific results. One can tell exactly what a sinner will do next. The same temptation coming to the same man has the same result. S. Paul said of himself, when he was living according to 'those things' : 'The good that I would I do not : but the evil which I would not, that I do.' But when his soul caught the vision of Christ, and fell in love with Jesus, he went off on all sorts of adventures. His old friends had been Pharisees, very much all of one pattern, but now all sorts of new and wonderful friends came into his life, Greeks and Romans, tent-makers and slaves.

If there is some accepted evil in our life, or we are living for ourselves, the end of 'those things' will be, at the best, the power to buy a house to die in, at the worst, shame : but the end of 'these things,' union with our Lord.

THE GRACE OF GIVING

'He gave them bread from heaven.'—S. JOHN vi. 31

WHEN God gives Himself to us in our Communion, with the gift of Himself He gives also the gift of being able to give. The Bread of Life was consecrated, broken, and given, and the bread of our life must be consecrated, broken, and given too. The gift of God is not so much the gift of privilege as the privilege of being able to give.

Many people are disappointed because their first fervour fades, but the Bread of God is given to us not for a picnic in a pleasant place, but to give us strength to go on over dry tracts, to climb steep hills, to endure great bitterness. It is not very hard to give oneself if the gift is appreciated, or shows certain signs of effectiveness in consequence of the donation of itself. But seeing that the Gift of God, the Bread of Heaven, was cast out of the city, the feeding upon that Bread should surely produce the power to give with simplicity, without either the fear of or calculation of consequences. We feed upon Him Who gives, in order that we ourselves may have the grace of giving.

The late Baron von Hügel, who was so sane and true a mystic, loved to use the expression, ' the given-ness of God.' The very desire for God that any soul has is a grace from God, and all our efforts towards God have their first beginning in this grace of the given-ness of God.

CONTEMPLATIVE PRAYER

'Looking upon Jesus.'—S. John i. 36

A REALLY great artist will look at his subject many more times than he will look at his canvas. The action of his hand will be small in comparison with the action of his thought, and his action will be wholly directed by his thought. All day he will be looking—looking at light and shadow, looking at form. In other words, his day will be spent in contemplation. When he puts his paint-brush on one side, he will never put his art on one side.

That gives us some interpretation of what prayer may be. Prayer will have much more silence in it than words, and when we leave our meditation we shall see in the scenes of daily life mangers and crosses, Christ and His Mother sitting on the doorstep or standing in the market-place. Contemplative prayer goes on through all life, and weaves itself into everything we say and think and do. Vocal prayer need never be long ; no prayer need ever be formal. It does not matter so much how long we spend on our knees in the morning as that we should get up in the morning to give our selves to God.

It does not matter very much where a life is lived, in a convent or a castle, on a bed of sickness or in radiant health. The thing that matters is that the life should be a given life. The way of our life, whatever it may be, must be our way of following our Lord Jesus Christ. Life is the great opportunity for loving ; loving is proved as we take each opportunity of giving ; the gift is not less accepted or acceptable that is given in pain and patience and marked with the sign of the Cross of Christ.

LOAVES AND FISHES

'Labour not for the meat which perisheth, but for that meat which endureth unto everlasting life.'—S. JOHN vi. 27

EVEN loaves and fishes, 'the meat that perisheth,' are in themselves creatures of God and the product of sacrifice. These loaves were barley loaves, the bread of the poor ; but no loaf, however common, is produced without a great deal of sacrifice. There has to be the working of the plough, the sowing of the seed, the reaping and the crushing of the grain, the fire and the baking of the bread. Though the fish were but the common fish of the lake, many a fisherman has laid down his life in his trade.

But things that are good in themselves may be used wrongly and become occasions of sin. Loaves and fishes may become things we quarrel about, or things we make idols of, or things we waste. The very phrase, ' loaves and fishes,' has become a synonym for selfishness, because our Lord said, ' Ye seek Me, not because ye saw the miracles, but because ye did eat of the loaves and were filled.' It is a terrible thing if God's good gifts become things to quarrel about, or idols which come between us and the Giver, or if we use them as if they were of no account and waste them. When this great miracle was wrought, our Lord said, ' Gather up the fragments that nothing be lost.'

If we bring the loaves and fishes to Christ, and are content that they should be broken as well as blessed, they become almost a sacrament. They become means of union, uniting us with God and one another. If we can but surrender ourselves, our possessions, our talents, our business, our trade, wholly to God, then He can bless the gift, however little it may be, and make it food for the many.

LIGHT IN A PRISON

'A light shined in the prison.'—ACTS xii. 7

LIFE is often very much of a prison to people ; it keeps them fettered. The victory that overcomes the prison-house of life is the light of faith : faith that God made us, that we are His children and our spirits are free, and, though we were in a dungeon, we could escape to God by a simple act of faith ; faith that the great Son of God took our nature upon Him, and came into the prison-house of this life, and made it a place where we could have life more abundant ; faith that we are allowed to feed upon His life at our altar, and that our life may be made one with His. We can turn days of difficulty into days of victory, and the little place wherein our lives are lived into a Nazareth where our labour for men may become our service to God.

There is another prison-house, and that is the prison-house of sin. If we fall into sin, we lose our spiritual consciousness and our sense of God. We cannot pray. All life becomes dark and oppressive and closed in. Into that prison-house of sin comes God's loving offer of forgiveness, and, if we accept it and make a true repentance, a light shines in the prison, and the chains fall from us.

In the prison-house of pain the light of faith interprets our sufferings and difficulties as our share in our Lord's Passion. When that difficult cross of pain is laid upon us, and we can only lie and suffer, there is this light, to know that Jesus was scourged and hung upon the Cross and died in the dark, and that the very strength that triumphed then can be communicated to us in the Blessed Sacrament.

THE SELF-OBLATION OF THE SOUL

'Lord, Thou knowest all things ; Thou knowest that I love Thee.'
S. JOHN xxi. 17

S. PETER's character, like many another, was a mingling of opposites. He was humble and presumptuous, cowardly and courageous. He could strike a blow for his Lord and yet deny Him. Sometimes he must have seemed to himself to be two people. His whole hope lay in the assurance that, in spite of his failures, his Lord could forgive him and recognize that he loved Him. We, too, have had our times of loyalty and our driftings towards dishonour. The soul may often be a puzzle to itself. Our hope is in our Lord's understanding love.

Our Lord gives the forgiven soul something to do for Him. He said to S. Peter, 'Feed My sheep.' However humble it may be, for the forgiven soul there is always some work of self-oblation. Just a life of quiet faithfulness is often a thing of greatest value for the welfare of Christ's Church. We are all linked to one another in life, and it is impossible that a life of loving penitence should not be for the welfare of the world.

S. Peter was not permitted to retire to a tranquil old age. His life, like his character, was full of lights and shades, and in the bright light of martyrdom God willed that he should glorify Him by his death. His last moments must have been full of thanksgiving that after all he had died faithful. Constant self-distrust, constant dependence upon our Lord, will win for the soul the grace of final perseverance. Spiritual self-reliance is a great danger. One of the great purposes of a life of prayer is to save us from it. 'Lord, Thou knowest all things ; Thou knowest that I love Thee,' may be the daily expression of the soul's humble self-oblation.

THE SACRIFICIAL ASPECT

'We have the mind of Christ.'—1 Cor. ii. 16

No one thought and talked about the Cross more than S. Paul. The sacrificial aspect of our religion was ever in his mind. All sin has come about through the perversion of free will. God has given us all free wills ; He cannot force them or they would not be free ; He cannot take them away or we should cease to be people.

God solved His own problem by, in the Person of His Son, taking a free human will and coming into this world of ours, and with that free will making at all times the perfect choice. It is a wonderful thing that the King of kings and Lord of lords should have chosen the lowly manger for His crib, that He should have chosen the life of a village carpenter, and the cross of shame as the occasion of His exit from this world. That represents the perfect choice of a perfect free will.

When we say that we are redeemed by the Cross or by the Blood of Christ, we have to beware of allowing ourselves to think that His Sacrifice can function for us apart from our own wills. We are really redeemed by the loyalty of His perfect will, of which the Cross and the shedding of His Precious Blood represent the supreme sacramental expression. Our wills have to become one with His will. His loyalty has made our own possible. When we speak about being redeemed by the Cross we mean two things : first of all, that a perfect Sacrifice has been offered and is ever pleaded for us before the Father ; and secondly, that our own human nature can so pass into union with that Sacrifice as to merit God's acceptance.

THE TRANSFIGURATION

'He was transfigured before them.'—S. Mark ix. 2

It is one thing to see beauty and another thing to understand the secret of beauty. Let us ascend the Mount of Transfiguration and kneel with the apostles and see the face of Jesus shining, and let us try to understand the secret of His beauty.

If we may dare to use such language, the face of Jesus shone because He had found that for which He had been seeking all His life. He had found the Father's will. All His life Jesus had been seeking His Father's will. When the Blessed Mother and S. Joseph found Him in the Temple, He was talking to the great Rabbis there about it. In His forty days of fasting in the wilderness He was seeking all the time to know it. Now He has spent the night in prayer, and that night was one of a succession of God knows how many nights of profound and perfect prayer. As a result of this prayer came His perfect choice ; as a result of that choice came the transfigured beauty of Jesus. He sees completely what the Father's will is : that out of the human nature He has taken shall shine forth over the ages and over the whole universe the revelation of Love ; and that that Love can only be shown by sacrifice, by going to the last length to which Love can go. In that long night of prayer on the mountain we may believe that all the circumstances that would surely lead up to Calvary became clear to Him, and He accepted them with His will. With His own will He chose the bitterest path a man can know. There is the secret of the beauty of our Lord's face as He was transfigured—the unutterable loveliness of His choice.

THE CLOUD

'There came a cloud overshadowing them.'—S. MARK ix. 7, R.V.

A GREAT thinker, Emmanuel Kant, once said that, when we come to know all things, we shall know that the Divine Author of the universe was as wise in the things which He hid as in the things which He revealed. It is a common experience of our life that there is a cloud about us. Even S. Paul, with his penetrating gaze, could only say that he saw ' through a glass darkly.'

The mystery of our Lord Jesus Christ is surrounded with clouds. We know Him by reading the four Gospels, but, though they are inspired books, they are not magical books, and we see Him in them veiled as in a cloud. We know Him by our own experience, but through what clouds must our experience try to pierce ! We know Him through the visions of saints, but their visions are not ours. The best of us only know Christ through a cloud.

Perhaps we have to go through a cloud to God because this discipline of perplexity best trains our character and shapes our soul. If we could see everything perfectly clearly, there would be no education. A second reason may be that thus we have a share in our Lord's Passion. Unless we enter into the cloud of His pain, we cannot really enter into the light of His love. Then it unites us with others in a great adventure. Others are going through a cloud too, and we can share with them our gleams of light, shoulder their burdens, and give them our pity when the cloud presses upon them very sorely. For these three reasons we can see an appointment of God in the discipline of perplexity, the cloud through which the soul has to pass to get to God.

JESUS ONLY

'And suddenly looking round about, they saw no one any more, save Jesus only.'—S. MARK ix. 8, R.V.

THE abiding light, the abiding strength, the abiding comfort is Jesus only. The one Word of God for this world of ours is Jesus, and Jesus only. There have been pagans who have ignored the existence of the soul, and there have been ascetics who have ignored the existence of the body, and both these beliefs lead to confusion. But the one religion which produces the perfect type of humanity is the Incarnational religion of Jesus Christ, which reveals both the body and the soul to be God's creation, complementary to one another.

It was Jesus only Who transfigured our idea of God. Our God is not the awful Jehovah speaking in thunder from some Sinai and proclaiming His word with earthquake and trumpet. Our God is the God Who speaks in the still small voice of conscience, and He has given us His perfect Word in Jesus Christ, Who is the incarnation of the perfect conscience, the Word not spoken in thunder from a cloud, but made flesh and dwelling here amongst us. We, who are incarnate spirits, shall learn to understand God as we learn to interpret the Incarnate Word of God in the power of the Spirit of God. The Spirit reveals the Son, the Son the Father. It is through Jesus only that we arrive at the true knowledge of God.

We all of us have our parts to play in building up the New Jerusalem. He, Who came down from the mountain of prayer, had to ascend the mount of sacrifice. The apostles had to realize that, if it was a wondrous thing to see Him transfigured on Mount Tabor, it was an even more wondrous thing to see Him disfigured on Calvary.

SMALL OCCASIONS: GREAT OPPORTUNITIES

'He that is faithful in a very little is faithful also in much.'
S. LUKE xvi. 10, R.V.

THERE are often great opportunities in the little things of life. An ordinary life may be quite extraordinarily romantic, because beneath the conventional clothes of the local tailor, and the daily progress along the pavement of the same dull streets, is going on all the while the spiritual movement of a soul, accepting or rejecting the beckoning of the Divine Ideal, following in one way or another the romance and adventure of a spiritual destiny.

When the greatest of all created beings, the Blessed Virgin Mary, first looked upon the Face of God, what she saw was just a little Child, born of her own pure travail ; when the boys and girls came down the street of Nazareth on their way home from school, and passed the carpenter's shop, the Divine Life was there amongst the sawdust and the shavings ; and when the thief on the gallows turned an eye of admiration upon the courage and undefeated love of his fellow-sufferer, there, in the very place of common execution, was the grandest of all sacrifices being enacted.

Little things bring great opportunities for a great love, and have been the steps of a heavenly ladder to the greatest of lives. A convent comes into being because some good women see how wonderful a thing silence can be ; a children's home grows about the idea of the joy of guiding developing lives. All quiet housework and care and arrangement of the garden may have their inspiration from Nazareth, ministry to the sick and courage in growing old find their hallowing and help from Calvary, and the patience of prayer its radiant fortitude from the vision of the Saviour on the Holy Mount.

OCCUPATION, PROFESSION, VOCATION

'In all thy ways acknowledge Him, and He shall direct thy paths.'
Prov. iii. 6

THERE are three ways in which we can look at what we do :
as an occupation, a profession, or a vocation. Roughly
speaking, our occupation is that which we do because we
think we will or because we have nothing better to do ;
our profession is that which we are paid to do. But our
vocation is that which we do because we believe the great
God, Who gave us our mind and intellect and affections and
every part of our being, is calling us to use all that He has
given us in harmony with Him, to glorify Him, and to
express His beauty in our life.

Our Lord had His times of recreation, when He went to
the marriage-feast at Cana or the house of His friends at
Bethany. But all the while He was doing the will of God.
His occupations were lifted to the level of vocation. He had
His profession. He was a carpenter, and doubtless a very
good carpenter. But His profession all the while was fulfilled
in obedience to, and to the glory of, His Father. Again, to
the Scribes and the Pharisees their religion was their profession, and to many people it is just an occupation, but our
Lord's religion was always a vocation. He went to His
prayer with a sense that He was called to it. He came from
His prayer with a sense that all His life was to be lived in
communion with His Father.

We must pray that our religion may never drop into being
occupation or profession, but that occupation and profession
and the whole of life may be lifted to the level of vocation,
that God's Holy Spirit ' may in all things direct and rule our
hearts.'

TRUE PEACE

'The things which belong unto thy peace.'—S. LUKE xix. 42

A SOUL may be in a state of unrest, indifference, false peace, or true peace. To take a parable : a man might have a picture and be bothered because he did not know its true value ; or he might have had it for years and not know if it had any value. Again, he might believe he had a good picture, but when he showed it to a great artist the expert might say, ' I am sorry to disappoint you, but it is not a good picture ' ; or he might feel sure he had a beautiful picture and the artist might confirm his judgement.

In the same way there are states of unrest, indifference, false peace, and true peace. We can escape from the first as we find the forgiveness of God. We can be redeemed from the second as the presence of God gives us a vision that makes our life real. We can be saved from the third as the wounds of Christ bring to our life the acceptance and not the evasion of the Cross. We pass to the fourth in the service and worship which give life its vocation and its true end.

The lover of God is like the true artist, who will go through any travail to attain to the beautiful thing which he longs to see, and cannot be content with anything less, which means that his art is the following of a loveliness which is for ever unfolding. In his following he finds his peace

GOD AND THE INDIVIDUAL

'Not one sparrow.'—S. MATT. X. 29, R.V.

WHAT our Lord set before Him was individual faithfulness. Nothing would do for Him instead of His own integrity. His care for His individual spiritual life is a marked feature of His life. Again, we notice His individual care for individuals—the woman of Samaria, Nicodemus, the rich young ruler, the apostles. Though He spoke to crowds, He never did anything to get a crowd, and He often sent people away. He escaped from the crowd more than once, and He sent His apostles away in a boat, preferring for them the storm-tossed sea to the contagion of the crowd. We see too His own individual trust in the Father—' Alone, yet not alone.' He felt that everything depended on this lonely individual sacrifice. ' I, if I be lifted up, will draw all men.'

The coming of the individual soul to God can have no other effect but the experience of penitence. If a man does not know what penitence means, he really does not know what it is to come to God through Christ or to see the Light of the World in the light of the Holy Spirit. We do not want to be sorry for what God has made—for our sex, our capacity, our temperament. The question is, ' How have I, being I, as an individual, borne my part ? '

Just as I am not one of the crowd to Christ, so He must not be one of the crowd to me. Our Lord cares for me with an individual love. He came to seek the penitent thief, not to scold him. Nothing can give Him greater joy than my penitence. Sorrow for sin means that I know that sin is alien to me, that love is alive, that I have hope in my heart.

THE TREASURE OF THE HEART

'Where your treasure is, there will your heart be also.'

S. MATT. vi. 21

WE should probably have put this saying the other way round, and said that where a man's heart is, there will his treasure be. But the heart is easy to deceive. We may persuade ourselves that our heart is devoted to somebody or something, and then, when certain things are touched, it will be proved that *they* are the real treasure and our heart is *there*. If people give up their religion because some one forgets them or slights them, it is shown that their real treasure is in being thought of and considered, and not in Jesus only.

We have before us the example of One Whose treasure was proved to be in His Father's will. Every earthly treasure was taken from Him, and it was manifest that He counted as His supreme treasure His union with the Father's will. Thus it was proved that that was where His heart was always. This thought is a great help, for it teaches us that the place where our heart is is not shown by feelings of comfort but by that which we would wish to be our treasure, and which we strive, with whatever difficulty, to keep inviolate.

If Jesus is our real treasure, nothing can touch our treasure, and all the sorrow and suffering of life will only prove more truly where our real treasure is, and the great world of reality, which we call heaven, will reveal to us that, whatever life may have robbed us of it never touched the true riches.

STORM AND CALM

'The Lord will give strength unto His people ; the Lord will bless His people with peace.'—Ps. xxix. 11

THE 29th Psalm pictures a storm passing over the city and shaking the cedars of Lebanon and then dying away into the wilderness. From the bulwarks of Jerusalem some watcher sees the storm passing over the country, and from the battlements of the Celestial City the watchers and the holy ones see the storms of our life, and know that they will pass.

If we have Jerusalem in our hearts, we shall be able to preserve peace in times of trouble, for there will be no doubt in our minds about the issue. The soul can retire to her interior castle and view with a certain indifference that which befalls her exterior setting. She herself is secure in the peace of God which passeth all understanding. It is clear, when S. Paul speaks of himself as ' troubled on every side, yet not distressed,' that he had learnt the secret of retiring into the inward citadel of peace. In all temptations, if the will holds on to the will of God in contrite love, the soul need never lose her peace. No temptation can separate us from our union with God. The will that is faithful preserves the interior life of the soul as in an impregnable fortress.

There are three dispositions of soul which may be the direct result of a time of trial. The first is lowliness of heart ; then singleness of aim ; and the simplicity of contrite love. The three together form that character of calm that marks the saints of God who have come triumphantly out of great tribulation.

LIVING WATERS

*'Ho, every one that thirsteth, come ye to the waters, and he that hath
no money ; come ye, buy, and eat.'*—Isa. lv. 1

In Isaiah vi we read of the great experience of a great
prophet. As he looked back over his life he said, ' In the
year that King Uzziah died I saw the Lord.' Uzziah was a
very able and vigorous ruler, and at the beginning of his reign
everything looked extremely prosperous, but towards the
end of it things went wrong. The great king committed
an act of sacrilege, offering incense in the Holy Place, and
was struck down with leprosy. The end of his life was a
time of gloom for himself and trouble for his kingdom. It
was just in that time, when things were at their darkest, that
Isaiah had his great spiritual experience.

It was in the barren years that the soul of Isaiah came to
the waters of life. It was this experience that enabled him
to make so joyfully his prophetic affirmation. It was when
the clouds of the Passion were darkening the sky, and the
time of His ministry, which had been in its beginning such
a triumph, was to end, as He most surely knew, in the
dereliction of Calvary, that our Lord cried aloud, ' If any
man thirst, let him come unto Me, and drink.' His promise
was the true fulfilment of Isaiah's prophecies. It may be
true for us also that just when outward things are darkest,
in our wilderness we may be shown the way to the well of
living waters.

CLOTHES : I

'The kingdom of God is not in word, but in power.'—I Cor. iv. 20

IT is a dangerous thing to judge people by their clothes : clothes may be very deceiving. Words are clothes and may be very showy, but there may not be much in the thought behind them, which is the reality of which they are the clothes. To God our thoughts are known, and the phrases which clothe them do not deceive Him.

In the story of the two people who went up to the Temple to pray, the Pharisee strode right up to the altar and stood there, and gave out a prayer which was magnificently clothed, as he told God of the great things he did. The poor publican, who thought he was not worthy to stand anywhere near this holy man, stood afar off in the shadows and beat his breast and said, ' God be merciful to me a sinner.' To God the simple honesty of the publican's prayer was more acceptable, for all the shabby clothing of its expression, than the embroidered sentences of the Pharisee's prayer. God sees these things apart. He judges the thought apart from the word.

None the less, clothing may be and should be altogether appropriate. In beautiful religious language, music, ritual, or architecture, and indeed all religious art, we may have the lovely clothing of a lovely thing, a perfect body wedded to a perfect soul. This is undoubtedly the will of God. But it is always of course the soul that matters, and either gives to the clothing meaning or makes it a mockery.

CLOTHES : II

'All the ways of a man are clean in his own eyes, but the Lord weigheth the spirits.'—Prov. xvi. 2

Actions are the clothing of motives, and motives are the souls of deeds. There may be an action with very magnificent clothes and yet a poor motive, and there may be a splendid motive which is very shabbily clothed. As our Lord watched the people giving alms to the Temple, He saw a rich man give his pounds, but He could only price the action as the giving of mites, so shallow was the motive dressed in the magnificent gesture of the flung coins. Then He saw a poor widow creep forward and drop two mites into the treasury, but His penetration priced the action as worth thousands of pounds, perhaps, for He saw that she had made a magnificent sacrifice of all that she had for the love of God. Under the humble clothing of her gift He saw the splendid generosity of one of His saints.

There often is a great discrepancy between the outward act and the inward motive, and yet there never need be any rivalry between the two. The material need never be at war with the spiritual. The lines of George Herbert, so often quoted, are altogether true : ' Who sweeps a room as for Thy laws, makes that and the action fine.' When the motive is beautiful, the sweeping of a floor becomes magnificent. We think how One swept the floor at Nazareth, how He knelt and washed the feet of sinful men. The lowly gesture was the splendid clothing of the amazing humility of God.

SENT

'There was a man sent from God, whose name was John. The same came for a witness, to bear witness of the Light, that all men through Him might believe.'—S. JOHN i. 6, 7

THOSE two verses teach us three vital truths : the source and origin of life, the purpose of life, and the glory of life.

What am I ? I am a man sent from God. That is a very great thing to believe. If I am confronted with some great difficulty or problem, because I am a man sent from God I have His power to draw upon. This is the very foundation of prayer : because I am a man sent from God I may speak to God, I must ask His counsel and take Him into my confidence. 'There was a man sent from God whose name was ——'—each one of us can put in his own name. The origin of life is divine.

What is the purpose of life ? Each one of us is sent that he may bear witness to the Light, to the fact that we *are* sent from God. We can bear witness through pain, and the mystery of pain may become a way of witnessing to the beauty of courage and faith. We can make this capital even out of our sins, that through our sorrow for them we witness to our love of God in true penitence. If we are sinned against, we can bear witness to our faith in God through our own forgiveness. Our lives, like that of S. John, are to be witnesses to the Light.

It is a glorious thing if, because of the way we live our life, other people become believers in life and the God Who gave us life. That is indeed to let our light so shine before men that, because of it, they glorify our Father which is in heaven.

SPIRITUAL DEPENDENCE

'Blessed are the poor in spirit ; for theirs is the kingdom of heaven.'
S. Matt. v. 3

We live in a peculiarly independent age, so perhaps there is special need to emphasize the fact that all Christians are called to a state of dependence upon God. As we contemplate our Lord, we see human nature in a right relationship to God, dependent upon God, and dependent upon Him in a life of deliberately chosen poverty and pain. The state of poverty will be a state of blessedness if it makes those who are poor depend upon God. The religious is of course called especially to emphasize by his vow of poverty this state of the absolute dependence of the creature upon the Creator. Religious Communities have always deteriorated in proportion to their forgetfulness of this. Reformers and founders have always been those who specially remembered and drew attention to the state of entire and absolute dependence upon God as the right and natural condition for those called to live the supernatural life.

The whole world is made up of beings dependent upon one another. All life is made up of relationships. Our first consciousness was that of dependence upon a mother, and all the blessings of life ever since have been the result of right relationships. All the evil of life, the agony of life, is in wrong or broken relationships. Every problem is a problem of relationships, of class to class, nation to nation, sex to sex, individual to individual. What does human progress mean but the bringing about of a better relationship between the units that make up humanity ? The Sacred Humanity of Christ ever kept this relationship of perfect dependence upon God, and through Him we can pass into that relationship of dependence, which will make us at the same time independent of the treatment of men and yet those upon whom they can wholly depend.

THE TESTING OF THE WILL

'Count it all joy when ye fall into divers temptations.'

S. JAS. i. 2

THIS surprising statement no doubt came out of S. James's own experience. The only way in which we can read joy into temptation is by taking it as being for the testing of the will, and that is surely what the apostle means. It has to be proved that we are doing right from the highest motives ; that we are doing right because it *is* right, and not because it is profitable ; that we are doing the true thing because it *is* true, and not because it is politic. There is an old story of the vision of a saint. He dreamt that he met an angel walking along bearing a pitcher of water in one hand and a brazier of coal in the other. When he asked the angel where he was going, the reply was : ' I am going to burn up heaven and to quench hell, in order that men may serve God with a pure intention.' This old story gives us a true thought. If we do right from thoughts of punishment or reward, we may be doing right things but we are not really doing right.

Every one of us shares the human nature that killed Christ, and we know therefore that we have tainted wills, wills that can make that fatal choice, the choice of being selfish. The redemption of human nature by God is not something worked outside us. It is the redemption of the will. Heaven is the sphere of redeemed wills. All our life we have to be tested, and if, through the experience and discipline of this life, and the purification of the life to come, our wills are redeemed, then because our will will be the same as the will of our Father in heaven we too shall be in heaven.

FOUND OUT

'By their fruits ye shall know them.'—S. MATT. vii. 20

WE find out what people are really like by the way they take the things that happen to them. One might think a woman very charming, and yet find her fail in the day of trouble ; or one might be with a man when a fire broke out at a theatre, and find that he was immediately in a panic ; or one might see some one, whom one had always regarded as very commonplace, do a very beautiful act. In each case one would say, ' Well, I never thought he or she was like that ! ' The circumstances of life reveal character.

Our Lord willed to come into this world and bring with Him nothing, to start with the poorest and to meet life as it came, and each thing as He met it revealed His character. Hate came to Him, and revealed His love. Success came to Him, and revealed His humility. Failure came, and revealed His faith. All things came to Him, eventually death, and death itself contributed to His royalty, for it revealed that He is alive for evermore.

Life finds us out, and our first discovery may be very like the discovery of S. Peter when he went out and wept bitterly after denying his Lord. But that was not the last word about Simon Peter, nor need our failures ever be the last word about ourselves. We can learn by our mistakes, and, if life finds *us* out, we can find out our God in our life, and through its challenge and His grace bring forth the fruit that shall make us known as His children.

HOW MUCH MORE

' If ye . . . how much more . . . your heavenly Father ? '
S. Luke xi. 13

The argument of this discourse is what logicians call an *a fortiori* argument. If imperfect people give good things to their children, how much more will the all-perfect Father give good gifts to His children!

Divine relationships are the foundation of human relationships, and human relationships are the symbol and expression of divine relationships. The reason there are human fathers and mothers is because God's love is creative. The reason why we can be friends with one another is because God is our friend. Why is it that the father will give his boy a bit of bread when he asks for it, and not a stone ? Because the fatherhood of the father is founded on the Fatherhood of God, and the exercise of this fatherhood is the symbol of the Divine Fatherhood.

In the words, ' Ask, and ye shall receive ; seek, and ye shall find ; knock, and it shall be opened unto you,' there is a simple truth enshrined, and that is that relationships ought to be put to the test. If a father has a naughty boy, that is the test of his fatherhood. From whom but his father should the boy who has got into trouble ask for sympathy and understanding ?

Our belief in the validity of the Christian Sacraments has for its foundation our belief in the character of God. If we ask for bread, will He give us a stone ? He is our Father ; He knows the needs of our souls. The security for the Sacraments of the Church is not the meticulous repetition of a certain formula, but the character of God, His knowledge of His children's needs, and His love to supply those needs.

THE POWER OF GOD

'He hath done all things well.'—S. MARK vii. 37

WE know what it is sometimes to see a number of people in great confusion. There is something to be done, and nobody likes to be the first to make a start. No one among them trusts himself, and there is no one the rest will trust, so all is confusion. Then some one appears who is master of the situation, confidence comes and a sense of assurance and power, as all are gripped and gathered together by a personality.

Now what in any number of given cases some one man may be, that Christ is to all the race and all the world. Jesus is the revelation of the power of God. The old story of Samson is not without its lesson, and should excite the imagination as we read it. What is the secret of the power of a great personality? Delilah sought it till she found it in Samson that she might make it of no avail. It is for us to seek the secret of the power of our God that we may find in it our salvation. Love is the secret of His power. Our Samson has been betrayed and His secret made light of, He has been blinded and bound and made the sport of Philistines. But though hate could kill Love, Love could, like Samson, in His death greatly prevail. Samson was content to die if a great multitude of Philistines died too ; our Lord was content to die alone that all mankind might find life. So like and unlike are the Old Testament story of the strong man and the New Testament revelation of the power of God's love.

THE WORK OF FAITH

*'Labour not for the meat which perisheth, but for that meat which
endureth unto everlasting life, which the Son of Man shall give
unto you.'*—S. JOHN vi. 27

HERE we get the contrast between what we do on our side
and what God does on His side. What we do is spoken of
as labouring, working. His attitude to us is always an attitude
of giving. He wants to give us His pardon, He wants to
give us Himself. We never have to *get* God to give. Our
work is the work of taking, but we have to get that attitude
of mind and will that wants to take what God is so anxious
to give. So often we are like the man with the muck-rake
in Bunyan's parable, who kept his eyes upon the ground,
while a shining angel was standing above him handing him
a heavenly crown, but he was too much occupied with his
groping in the muck-heap to see.

' What work shall we do ? ' said the people to our Lord,
and He replied, ' Believe on Him Whom God hath sent.'
Our work is this believing, this faith. When the people
asked for a sign from heaven, they were shown a work on
earth. That work was to bring their minds to the contemplation of Christ, to exercise their faith by receiving His
promises and obediently fulfilling His commands. He said, 'I
am the Bread of Life : he that cometh unto Me shall never
hunger ; he that believeth on Me shall never thirst.' God's
very nature is a self-giving, but we have, by faith, to take.
The coming to God includes all the activities of our life.
' He that cometh unto Me '—that expresses every exterior
activity. ' He that believeth '—that expresses every interior
activity. But this coming is not a small thing. It is indeed
a labour for the ' meat which endureth unto everlasting life.'

LIVING BREAD

'Whoso eateth My Flesh, and drinketh My Blood, hath eternal life.'
S. JOHN vi. 54

WE cannot eat anything that has not had life in it : we cannot eat stones. When we feed upon material food, what we eat has to have had life, whether vegetable or animal, and that life has had to be sacrificed. We are feeding on something really that laid down its life for us. But it was a lower life than our life, and it became incorporated into a body that will ultimately die, and so entered into the process of dying.

The feeding upon God in the Blessed Sacrament is exactly the opposite, although the feeding on material food is a parable of that higher feeding, because what we feed on does nourish us, and our Catechism tells us that 'our souls are refreshed by the Body and Blood of Christ as our bodies are by the Bread and Wine.' But when we come to feed upon our Lord at His altar, upon a Life that has been sacrificed for us, it is a Life higher than our own, and we do not so much take that Life into our life as we are taken into that Life. Instead of taking into us, as we do when we have our ordinary food, a lower life which becomes part of our dying life, we are taken into a higher life than our own and become united with an eternal life.

We must labour for this heavenly food. Our feeding upon earthly food goes on without any particular act of will, but this feeding upon the life of God is a process which has to call into being all our devotion, all our self-oblation, all our self-surrender, that we may be taken up into that Divine Life which never dies.

LOYALTY TO MAN

'And Ruth said, Intreat me not to leave thee, or to return from following after thee : for whither thou goest, I will go . . . the Lord do so to me, and more also, if ought but death part thee and me.'—RUTH i. 16, 17

IN this passage we are told of the loyalty of one woman to another. It represents the perfect loyalty of a woman to a woman, of a friend to a friend. Every one of us is probably very loyal to some one, but what we want to learn is to make our loyalty to our particular friend a standard of loyalty to every one else. The woman you care for most is the representative to you of all other women, the man you care for most is the representative of all other men. The way in which you behave towards the race should be the way in which you would wish to behave to your best friend. Our Lord came into this world as a representative man, and pointing to the men and women in the market-place He said : ' Behold My mother and My sister—behold My brethren ' ; and again He said, 'Inasmuch as ye have done it unto one of the least of these My brethren, ye have done it unto Me.'

We can only get this kind of loyalty as we learn loyalty to God, and we have to learn our loyalty to God from His loyalty to us as revealed in the Incarnation. God, the Eternal Love, has created us, and we have gone astray. But our disloyalty to Him only drew forth the revelation of His faithfulness to us, proved by the Manger, the Cross, and the Altar.

LOYALTY TO GOD

'Thy people shall be my people, and thy God my God.'

In our Lord, as He represents us as Man, we see the perfect loyalty of a human will to the Divine Will. In the temptation in the wilderness, in the patience at Nazareth, in the ministry in Galilee, in the agony in the Garden, we see the steady progress of that loyalty to the test of its perfection upon the Cross. There on Calvary is revealed perfectly the Father's will, because the human will of Christ is completely one with that will. In the Incarnation the divine idea of a human life is revealed for all time, because there is no difference between our Lord's exposition of a human life and the divine idea of a human life.

The Church is the company of all faithful people who are following their Lord, and are being taught more and more by His Spirit the cost and the splendour of loyalty to Him. As they learn to be loyal to Him, so they learn to be loyal to one another after the pattern of that loyalty. When we come to the altar of Christ, we come to the Lord Who was loyal to the disloyal, faithful to the unfaithful, and we take in through union with Him the power to go on alone and in darkness in this supremely costing way. The people of His love become our people, His Father's will our will, and so these lovely words that come to us over the ages, as one woman on life's lonely road was loyal to another, may mystically express our own faith and loyalty to our Lord and His people.

THE GOOD SAMARITAN

'*When he saw him, he was moved with compassion, and came to him.*'

S. LUKE x. 33, R.V.

OUR Lord loved to teach people by painting word pictures, and in the parable of the Good Samaritan He paints a picture of the love of God.

Humanity is as a man who has fallen among thieves and been robbed, and left there incapable of saving himself. We feel we have been foolish, that we have been robbed, that we cannot save ourselves. We have been robbed by our own stupidity. This man ought not to have been travelling alone.

The first person who comes along is the priest, who may stand for formal religion. Formal religion passes by and leaves humanity where it is. Then comes a type we know very well, the good-natured person who comes and looks at the man, and goes away and leaves him. Many people do that. They discuss the troubles of life and look at the slums, and go away and leave them.

Then the Samaritan passes by and comes where the man is. In that sentence is told all the deep mystery of our Lord's Incarnation. He came down to be in the poverty of the poor. He did not pass by, He did not come down and look at it, and then go back to heaven. He did not come to tempted men and say, 'You ought not to have that temptation,' but He came to where the tempted man was. He came into the place of suffering, and willed that His own coronal should be a crown of thorns. The story of the Good Samaritan is the story of the Incarnation. It is a picture of the love of God.

130

THIEVES

'A certain man went down from Jerusalem to Jericho, and fell among thieves.'—S. Luke x. 30

SOMETIMES people have an idea that religion robs us of something, that being religious means saying good-bye to a good time. They think that they have to choose between a good time here and a bad time hereafter, or a bad time here and a good time hereafter. Our Lord teaches us exactly the opposite. He came that we might have life more abundantly. There is only one kind of good time, and that is doing God's will. There is only one universe, God's universe ; one everlasting law, God's will ; one everlasting joy, God's love ; and one everlasting peace, God's heaven. Everything that tries to draw us away from that faith is the real thief.

There are three chief thieves that rob us : idleness, ignorance, and impurity. Idleness robs people of effort and development ; unemployed people are being robbed of their true self-expression as men. Ignorance is a thief ; people are always being robbed through ignorance of riches that ought to be theirs. Again, impurity is a thief ; it persuades people that a sensation which lasts for a moment is the true riches, and all the while impurity is robbing them of their peace and their communion with God.

To the man who has fallen among these thieves comes the Good Samaritan. To the man who has fallen among the thieves of idleness He brings work, and shows that life is a vocation. To the man who is ignorant, who does not know what life is for, Jesus comes as the Light of the World, and tells him that he is a son of God. To the man whose eyes are blinded by impurity the good Lord comes with eye-salve, that he may be saved from lust as he learns to see the vision of the true Love.

THE FRUIT OF THE SPIRIT : I

'The fruit of the Spirit is love, joy.'—GAL. v. 22

THE perfect fruit of the Spirit of God is the Incarnation of our Lord, and we may consider S. Paul's words in the light of that revelation.

When we think of the great God entering the universe which He created, how wonderful is the ritual of the stable and the straw ! The fruit of the Spirit is manifest in the love of Jesus lying in the manger. As we think of Him going through life, He did not draw clever people to Himself by argument or have a great organization. The fruit of the Spirit is shown in love, this perfect love which appeals to love, and those who love Love come to Love ; they are simple folk, very stupid some of them, but they gather round Him as He passes on His way from the manger to the shop and along the roads of Galilee, till at last He climbs the lonely hill—the fruit of the Spirit shown in love all the while.

The second fruit of the Spirit, says S. Paul, is joy. We speak of our Lord Jesus Christ as the Man of Sorrows, and He Himself spoke of having nowhere to lay His head, and then, without the slightest sense of incongruity, He said, ' Come unto Me, all ye that labour and are heavy-laden, and I will give you rest.' No one has ever suggested that He was saying something far-fetched and extravagant, or disputed His power to give rest. Again, on the night of His betrayal He prayed for His apostles that they might have His joy. How could He speak of joy, He Who was going out to betrayal and torture ? Because His joy is the joy of the Spirit, and the joy of the Spirit is the very spirit of joy.

THE FRUIT OF THE SPIRIT : II

'The fruit of the Spirit is . . . peace.'—GAL. v. 22

THE third 'fruit of the Spirit' of which S. Paul speaks in his letter to the Galatians is peace. The fruit of the Spirit is a threefold peace.

First, peace in oneself, as one has surrendered to the highest thing one knows, the peace of a perfect integrity. Our Lord could not be bribed or frightened into taking some lesser way than the way of complete holiness, so that He knew a perfect peace in Himself. Secondly, there is peace in our relation to God. We can always have peace, because the whole revelation of God is that He is always ready to forgive the very moment that we come to Him. If we have done wrong and want to start again, we can, here and now. We can be quite sure that the wish to do the new right thing is His own gift, His own hand held out to us, His own prevenient grace. Thirdly, we can have peace in our relations to other people, because people cannot stop our loving them. People laid traps for our Lord and plotted against Him, but nothing lessened His love for them. When they were actually hammering nails into His hands and feet, He was still praying for them. There is the supreme flowering of the Spirit in the peace of that prayer.

We may know great agony in our body, great agony in our mind, and yet thereby make perfect the joy of the spirit. If we yield ourselves to the inflow of the Spirit of God, the Incarnation reveals to us that the fruit of that Spirit will be love, joy, and peace.

LED

WE are all being led, whether we like to admit it or not, and we are all in some way leading others, because we cannot help influencing people by the way in which we live ourselves. We ought to think seriously by what spirit we are led.

S. Paul, writing about the flesh and the spirit, says: 'These are contrary the one to the other.' We cannot believe that God has made two things that are in their essence contrary to one another, but if we think it out we see that these things are not contrary in their essence but in their rivalry for leadership. The body is the most excellent servant, but the most terrible master. What we have to see to is that we are never led by our bodies, but that we are so led by the Spirit of God that our spirits express themselves through our bodies in union with His will.

How are we to know whether we are being led by the Spirit of God ? Spirits can come to us in disguises. We are told that the devil can disguise himself as an angel of light, and we cannot imagine him dressing himself up as anything else to spiritual souls. If we are to be sure, we must have the desire to be led by the Spirit of God, and we must pray to Him that we may be so led. We do really know in the deep of us when we are led by His Spirit, and as we are loyal to that leading we shall understand more and more the doctrine of Christ, Who, as He hangs upon the Cross in our human nature, is for ever the sacrament of perfect loyalty to the Spirit of God by which He was led.

SLOWNESS AND SWIFTNESS

'One day is with the Lord as a thousand years, and a thousand years as one day.'—2 S. Pet. iii. 8

There are two characteristics about the work of the greatest artists, slowness and swiftness. Great artists are patient men ; they spend much labour in developing their sense of perception ; they spend long hours in making studies. Again, the great artist is exceedingly swift : a dexterous touch here, a touch there, makes all the difference. It seems as though the picture arrives by magic. It is swift because it is so sure, and it is sure because the preparation for it has been so slow.

God, the great Artist and Author of our life, is no exception to this rule. We see His slowness, His patience, creatively in the principle of evolution, redemptively in the ' spiritual remnant' of which the prophets speak. We see His swiftness and sureness of touch in the conversion of some saint, as when S. Matthew rose a new man, as the light smote upon him when our Lord said, ' Follow Me ' ; or in the emergence of some new type ; or in the quick possession of a lesser thing by a higher and more spiritual power, as when life possesses matter, or reason possesses life. Above all, we see it when He Himself took a human nature—' While all things were in quiet silence, and that night was in the midst of her swift course, Thine Almighty Word leaped down from heaven out of Thy royal throne ' (*Wisd.* xviii. 14, 15). God, the great Artist, is slow and swift, but He is always sure.

In our lives there must be these things. We must know slowness in learning, all the slow patience that follows in the dim wake of dying light left by a vision that has passed. But, in the fullness of time, all swiftly will come the sight that sees the vision of God.

SPIRITUAL VISION

'God is a Spirit : and they that worship Him must worship in spirit and truth.'—S. JOHN iv. 24, R.V.

WE all have a consciousness of spiritual beauty. It is part of the experience of prayer to develop this consciousness and to follow the light which it brings. As we follow it, so our capacity for vision increases. Prayer is faith in our own capacity for spiritual vision, and exercise of that capacity. Teaching is faith in the capacity of other people for spiritual vision, and appeal to that capacity.

Our Lord had amazing faith in people's capacity for spiritual vision. When He spoke to that poor, smirched woman of Samaria, He said to her some of the most profound spiritual truths He ever said to any one. It was to her He said, ' God is a Spirit, and they that worship Him must worship Him in spirit and in truth.' He shared with her His own vision of the spiritual kingdom, which was not fettered to Jerusalem or to any place, but into which all spiritual people could enter by the adventure of faith.

In Acts x we read of two people who had visions, Cornelius a disciple, and Peter a teacher, and to both these men the vision came when they were at prayer. Cornelius had his vision of the man who was to come to teach him. Peter had his vision of the equality of souls in the sight of God, a vision that broke down his race and class prejudices. The beginning of the Catholic Church was the breaking down of Jewish prejudice, the idea of the God of the nation giving place to belief in the God of the world. It was the appeal of one who had capacity for spiritual vision to another who had that capacity. The vision came to the teacher and to the disciple, and to both the vision came at their prayer.

FROM PUBLICAN TO SAINT

'At the place of toll.'—S. MATT. ix. 9, R.V.

ONCE to a man at the place of toll, bending over his business, getting the best material gain he could out of his day's work, came the vision of a face, which smote upon his soul in such fashion that his life could never be the same again. He saw the face of Jesus, and with that vision came an uplift transfiguring life and giving it purpose and direction.

A man's life is altogether affected by the vision of God which he has. Our Lord's conflict with the Pharisees lay in this, that He had one vision of God and they another. Christ Himself is the one true vision of God, but people can have very different ideas of Christ. Just as it is only the real Christ Who can reveal the Father, so it is only the Holy Spirit Who can reveal the Christ. As long as a man is honestly trying to interpret in his life the Christ of his own conscience, the mistakes he makes will ultimately bring him to reality. He is learning all the while. But if a man sees one Christ with his conscience and interprets another with his life, he is killing in himself all power of vision and harming in some degree the spiritual sense of his generation. The sin of the Christian is to see one Christ and to reproduce another.

The test of our lives lies in this—in the word that we leave behind us. Each life is a word, each one of us is the revelation of a faith or a futility. S. Matthew left a Gospel behind him. Matthew the publican revealed what his life might have been if Jesus had never come into it ; S. Matthew the martyr-evangelist revealed what meeting with Jesus could mean.

THE KINGDOM OF GOD

'Seek ye first His kingdom, and His righteousness ; and all these things shall be added unto you.'—S. MATT. vi. 33, R.V.

THE first and most important step in the spiritual life is to desire to live a spiritual life. It is so easy to say, it is so hard to do. Splitting our text up and taking the words separately, in those two words, ' Seek first,' we get the thought of the deliberate direction of the will, the mind, the affections, towards God and the things of God. We may take the word ' ye ' as marking the individuality of the call. Each one of us as an individual is called in his own particular way to seek the kingdom of God and His righteousness. ' His kingdom ' stands for the complete dominance of God in every department of life. What we are to seek is not our convenience, not even our happiness, but His righteousness.

But the end is a fulfilling, not a thwarting. The last words of the passage are, ' and all these things shall be added unto you.' Our Lord did not come to crush things but to claim them. Because we have sought first of all our Father and His will and His righteousness, we receive the great gifts of life from His hands with His benediction. We have not, so to speak, crept into the garden of God to steal flowers, but we have gone to God Himself, and He takes us into His garden and gives us the best flowers and the fruit.

So often we put ourselves first, and our friends second, and God a very bad third. If we put God first, and others second, and ourselves a very bad third, that will be the true order. If He really is first, then all our life and our comradeships will be transfigured and made worthy to be a part of His kingdom.

OUR GOD AND KING

'The Lord God omnipotent reigneth.'—Rev. xix. 6

EVERY part of the universe must be the kingdom of God. There cannot be more than one God, one supreme and ultimate King, and His Kingship must extend to life's farthest limit. If there was one fragment of the universe of which He was not really the King, God would not be God. There may be rebellion, there may be disloyalty. It is clear that in parts of the universe, especially in the wills of men, God's supremacy is not recognized, and where He does not hold full sway there is distress and unrest. That reveals that those bits of territory are not perfectly governed, and that is so because they have not been brought under the supreme authority of the true King. Where we give our will in loyalty and allegiance to our Sovereign King, there is the kingdom of God, and there is the peace of those that dwell therein.

And, oh, what a rest there is in the knowledge that God is the supreme Sovereign of His universe, Whose will must inevitably triumph. 'The Lord God omnipotent reigneth'— not myself or any creature, but God the Creator, the Redeemer, the Leader, reigns. We are His product, and however much we may have marred His creation, He has redeemed us with a mighty redemption, and that end for which He created us is possible for us. However much we may have failed or fallen, we can come to Him to start afresh. He has made the highest possible for us by redemption, He will lead us to the highest by inspiration, for He would set us in the very place where we can best fulfil His will and interpret His love, our very own place in the kingdom, for His love has a place for the least of us.

THE COMING OF THE KINGDOM

As God is everywhere, so is His kingdom everywhere. But there are tracts and territories that are not under the dominion of their rightful King, and that is what is meant by sin. Men are always trying to find satisfaction in creatures, but where they give their first allegiance to created beings the result is an inevitable disappointment, and that disappointment is a symptom of their disloyalty or their divided allegiance. Where then should be the remedy, and how is the recovery to be accomplished, and the true reign of the King of Love brought about ? The remedy will be in the life of faith, but real faith in God will not be shown by being content with things as they are.

In a certain sense no Christian can ever be contented. There must be a divine discontent in the soul of every saint, for we can never stay where we are. We are always being called to higher service, and God is always seeking to show us higher revelations of beauty. Nor, again, will the victory be won by trying to fight a wrong in any way but God's way. It is always our temptation to try to overcome evil with evil. It is so very difficult to try to overcome evil with good. Again, the remedy will not come by ignoring the conditions of life and shutting oneself away from the rest of the world in a quiet corner of one's own. Faith in God will be shown by claiming the whole of life, science, labour, art, sex, everything, as God's kingdom. The Church must claim the world, for the kingdom of God will only come when the Church and the world are one.

THE KING'S PRIVY CHAMBER

'The kingdom of God is within you.'—S. LUKE xvii. 21

ONE might be at the King's court among those who paid him honour, or in his council chamber with those who presented him with petitions for the general good, but if one wanted to ask something touching one's own private need, it would be in the King's privy chamber that one sought him. Our Lord has taught us to judge of heavenly things by earthly analogies, and this little parable may help us to think more clearly of our secret intercourse with God in the privy chamber of our own soul. What our soul is to our body His presence is to our soul, and there in the secret place of our own soul we may seek for God. We have access to this privy chamber of our King, since He has given us the key, which is our own free will.

If we would have audience with the King, we must enter that chamber quite alone, but we may come as we are, humbly, simply, and obediently, and the King, like all great men, will give us His whole attention. When we pray, we want to do our best to be absolutely and utterly alone with God. That is why silence is so profoundly important in a retreat, and why that deepest silence, the silence of desire, is so important.

Prayer does not mean getting God to do things, but co-operating with Him in doing things. It is not reminding God of things He has forgotten, but reminding oneself that God is remembering, and the way in which God is remembering somebody may be by giving us the prevenient grace which made us set about praying. It was because God remembered first that we began to pray. It was because God was there first that we came to pray.

THE KING'S FACE

'His servants . . . shall see His face.'—REV. xxii. 3, 4

OUR Lord came to reveal the God Whom eye hath not seen, and in the mirror of our Lord's life and revelation we can, though under a veil, look upon the face of our King.

She who first saw the King's face looked upon a little Child, and those who are led to found crêches and work at children's hospitals and child welfare have seen the face of God in a little child.

The boys and girls of Nazareth, the men who carried boats to the shore, the men who came to Him that He might fashion the yoke for their oxen, saw the face of God in a carpenter at His work. He is the Lord of Labour, and the common work of every day may be the divine employ of God Himself. Those who seek to bring help and comradeship and beauty into the life of the factory and the shop and the street have seen the face of God in the Carpenter of Nazareth.

Since God mingled His life with our life, and knew our temptations, and in loneliness sought the way of holiness, so every one who strives to keep a pure ideal and bring purity and chivalry and truth into life has seen the face of God in the tempted Christ.

Again, since He suffered torture of mind and soul and body, those who see human suffering and long to succour it, who themselves accept suffering and seek to sanctify it, whose sympathy compels them to go amongst the suffering, have seen the face of God crowned with thorns.

Lastly, those who have felt the compelling call of God to come apart, who have felt there is nothing so worth while as prayer, have seen the face of Christ in prayer on the Mount of Transfiguration.

CONTACT WITH CHRIST

*'And when the Lord saw her, He had compassion on her, and said
unto her, Weep not.'*—S. LUKE vii. 13

THE first thought that this story suggests is that whenever
Jesus really meets some one, something happens. Here are
two streams of people : the stream of common human
experience, sorrowing people carrying the dead body of a
young man, who was the only son of a widow, and the stream
of people following Jesus into the city. The two meet, and
our Lord beholding the poor mother has compassion on her.
The miracle happens : He gives her back her treasure.

There are three resurrections that our Lord Jesus wrought:
that of the daughter of Jairus who was just dead, that of this
boy who was being carried out to be buried, and that of
Lazarus who had lain in the sepulchre three days. There
was an ascending scale of wonder, possibly to teach us that
nothing is beyond the power of our Lord. What is true of
the body is true also of the soul. There is no soul so corrupt
that it cannot be brought back if it is brought into contact
with Jesus. From any deadness there may be a resurrection
to the wonder of life and service.

This story gives us a true revelation about prayer. Prayer
is something much wider than we think, something more
than saying words. That woman did not ask our Lord
to raise her boy, but her sorrow was to Him a prayer and
had one of the three greatest answers to prayer that there
have ever been. Our sorrow about our own souls, about
our Church, or for some one else's need, is itself a prayer,
and when Jesus sees us He has compassion upon us, and our
prayer is beginning to be answered already.

SPIRITUAL CONSCIOUSNESS

'Lord, I pray Thee, open his eyes, that he may see.'
2 KINGS vi. 17

THIS is a beautiful story of Elisha the prophet and his servant in the beleaguered city. The young man thinks the city is doomed, and he and his master with it. He looks at Elisha and sees that he is wholly calm and untroubled, and he cannot think why. Then Elisha prays to God that his servant's eyes may be opened, and he gets a new consciousness   He is aware of spiritual presences around him, and he enters, if only for a moment or two, into that mysterious consciousness of the spiritual world which was the possession of that man of prayer and fasting and spiritual prowess, the prophet Elisha.

There are degrees of physical consciousness, and many things about us which we could see or hear if we had a higher degree. A scientific expert made a musical instrument with a very high note, so high that a human being could not hear it ; but when it was sounded near a horse, the horse pricked its ears immediately. The purely mechanical apparatus of the microscope will enable us to see wonders that our eyes in their natural condition are incapable of seeing.

Now what an animal is given in the purely physical way, and what a microscope can do for us in a purely mechanical way, our religion can do for us in a spiritual way. We can get new faculties through our religion, a new spiritual consciousness. To ordinary vision the events of the Passion were complete failure and catastrophe. To the spiritual eyes of our Lord they were something altogether different— the cup which His Father gave Him to drink, love's perfect vocation. Spiritual eyes, which prayer has purified, will enable us to see in every challenge of life the vocation of God.

THE TRUE SOCIALISM

'Fellow-citizens.'—Eph. ii. 19

WE are ' members one of another,' we are fellow-citizens.
We cannot get away from that fact. All sorts of fellow-
citizens take their share in providing our Sunday dinner.
Our lives affect the lives of other people. We can make
them happy or unhappy ; we can render them service or
injury. If we do wrong, we injure others. If we do nothing
at all, we are not pulling our fair share in the boat. There
are some people who produce slums, who get pleasure at the
cost of other people's pain and shame. We do not want to
be fellow-citizens with them. We want to be fellow-citizens
of the saints, to give the best we can in this Church of God
in which we are all born free.

If we really believe that God is always with us, how it
will transfigure our lives ! How it will transfigure the
journey in the bus, the work in the office, if all the while
we are thinking, ' Here am I, having contact with God.
Inasmuch as I do kindness to these people, I am ministering
to Him : inasmuch as I receive kindness from them, I am
receiving it from Him. This mixing up with my fellow
human beings is a sacred thing. This office is Nazareth,
this street is a street of Galilee.' There stands One among
us Whom so often we do not know. Then somebody's
face shines, we see a soul through the eyes and a Presence
through the soul. All our life, in our home, in our work,
in our street, becomes a tremendously exciting thing, because
God is always there, just such a little veil between us and
Him. That is the true Socialism, the true transfiguring of
life, the knowing Him in our brother.

SPIRITUAL CAPITAL

'Labouring fervently for you in prayers.'—Col. iv. 12

THERE are laws in the spiritual life as there are in the natural life. If we do not put money into the bank, we have no money to take out. If we do not really pray, we have no spiritual power. The temptation comes to do a passionate or a cowardly thing, and we do it. We are bound to do it, if we have not the spiritual wealth we need. If a man has a hundred pounds in the bank, and simply lives on it, it will not take him long to get to the end of it, and when he presents a cheque the bank says, ' We cannot give you anything, because you have nothing to take out.' If we live on capital, there comes a day when we have no wealth behind us to meet the claims we have to meet. The only remedy for such a state of things is to create wealth by labour, whether of mind or muscle.

The same thing is true of the spiritual life. The conditions of life are always making demands upon us. To-morrow something may come which will try our temper or challenge our courage. There comes a sudden demand to be patient, and we are impatient. Something tempts us to tell a lie and we do. Why ? Because we are spiritually bankrupt, and make a demand upon a capital that does not exist. Our spiritual bank is empty. That is the real root trouble of the Church : that is why there is a shortage of money, a shortage of priests. When S. Paul talks of Epaphras labouring fervently for the Colossians in his prayers, he tells of one who is putting spiritual capital into the bank. That we may have spiritual capital to draw on, we must labour fervently in our prayer.

THE LOVE OF GOD

'Neither death, nor life, . . . nor height, nor depth, nor any other creature, shall be able to separate us from the love of God, which is in Christ Jesus our Lord.'—ROM. viii. 38, 39

THERE are three things we can remember about the love of God. First, it is prevenient. The fact that we can love God is due to the fact that He has loved us, and His love awoke in us that response to His love which is itself His gift. Even the pagan poets glimpsed this in their thoughts about their pagan deities. Juvenal says : *Carior est illis homo quam sibi*—'Dearer is man to them than to himself.' Surely while writing of his ancient gods, he was having a vision of ' the God and Father of our Lord Jesus Christ.' Before ever we thought of God He thought of us. S. Bernard used to say to his monks : ' Rise you never so early, God is before you, and you can never come into the chapel without finding Him waiting there.'

Secondly, nothing we can do can alter His love. God's love is wounded by our sin, but in no way affected in its intensity and its reality. He will never love us less because we hate Him. If a person sings out of tune, it does not put the piano out of tune. It has no effect whatever upon the piano or the eternal laws of harmony. Nothing can alter the love of God. What must be altered is our relationship to that love.

The third thing about the love of God is that it abideth ever. The love of God is the principle of the true happiness of all life, as the will of God is the principle of its existence. God is the supreme good of all His creatures ; from the smallest fragment of creation to the Blessed Mary and the greatest archangel, all find their joy in Him.

A THREEFOLD COMING : I

'God hath visited His people.'—S. LUKE vii. 16

THE Jews alone of all nations had the conception of God as One and Holy, and a tradition of an intercourse of God with His people, through a direct revelation of Himself to the individual, through the prophetic appeal to the conscience, and by His providential leading of the nation as a whole.

Abraham, Jacob, Joseph, Moses, Samuel, David, Daniel—what a wonderful tradition it is ! A long line of men following one another, convinced of the truth that ' God hath visited His people.' Every one of those men was marked by this distinctive character, that his life was a vocation, that he was sure that all prosperity based upon neglect of God was delusive and no suffering based on obedience to the will of God could issue in anything but peace and blessing. There was that recognition of God's intercourse with His people which was direct and spiritual. This conviction was often tried very sorely, sometimes profoundly shaken and by some forsaken, but always held most firmly by the prophets and the best of the people.

Again, there were those recognized as prophets, because their personal intercourse with God was believed in. Then there were what are called theophanies, mysterious supernatural appearances of angelic beings, occurring rarely to few people on particular occasions, but believed in with great conviction and not to be explained away. So those people who lived before our Lord came knew of an intercourse of God with men, through prophets and theophanies, which we may call incarnational, all affirming the truth that God hath visited His people.

Lastly, there was that tradition which began with the primitive altar put up in places where men had realized some special mercy of God, and was developed into the Church of the wilderness, the Tabernacle, and afterwards the Temple.

A THREEFOLD COMING : II

'Blessed be the Lord God of Israel ; for He hath visited and redeemed His people.'—S. LUKE i. 68

IN the fullness of time our Lord came, and God had intercourse with men in the Incarnation. Very God of Very God, for our sakes He became Very Man. In those wondrous three-and-thirty years when God lived on earth, when men could touch His human hand and touch God, when they could behold the calm scrutiny of human eyes and look in the face of God, when they could hear from the tenderest of human voices the words of God, they had intercourse with Him again in a spiritual way, an incarnational way, and a sacramental or ' Church ' way. He led His apostles into retreat to pray, He revealed God through His own incarnate self-revelation, and He formed a group of people into a Church.

Since our Lord ascended into heaven, and we live under the dispensation of the Holy Spirit, God's intercourse with us is not along different lines from those of old. We have our own spiritual experience : as we kneel in prayer, we can have direct intercourse with God, we are wrapped round with God, in Him we live and move and have our being. We have our incarnational experience ; as we minister to the least of Christ's children, we minister to Him ; as we receive light and healing and blessing from any of Christ's saints, we receive ministry from Him. We are also baptized into His Body, the Church, and that word ' Body ' is much more than a metaphor. It enshrines an idea. A body functions for the expression of a mind and personality. God has intercourse with us through the Body of Christ, the Holy Catholic Church. He has intercourse with us directly in our prayer, incarnationally in our fellow men, and through the divine society, the Body of Christ.

149

A THREEFOLD RESPONSE

'A threefold cord is not quickly broken.'—Eccles. iv. 12

Every Christian always, whether he realizes it or not, is being helped either through his own prayer, through the goodness of other people, or through the effect of Church services and Catholic tradition. ' A threefold cord is not quickly broken,' and if one strand of the cord should be frayed, it is a mercy that there remain two others. God's intercourse with us is spiritual, incarnational, and sacramental. That was the case before our Lord came, during His Incarnation upon earth, and is the case with us now. As God has intercourse with us, so we must seek to have intercourse with Him.

We must take trouble to cultivate spiritual intercourse with God. We should try sometimes to sit quietly and think : ' God made me : this body of mine was made by Him that it should express His own thought : my mind was made that I might think in communion with Him : my will was meant to choose His will. My whole being may have, here and now, complete and perfect union with my God.' That is spiritual communion with God. Then we can have intercourse with God incarnationally. Our Lord has told us that what we do to one of the least of our brethren, we do to Him. We can minister to Him in the poor and homeless, the sinful and the outcast, and we can receive ministry from Him in His saints. Lastly, our surest intercourse with God is our sacramental intercourse. The Church is the secure means of communion with God, a communion that depends for its security upon His fidelity to us rather than our fidelity to Him. The effect of this sacramental intercourse with Him will be not only spiritual communion, but should issue in Christian charity.

HARVEST

'Pray ye therefore the Lord of the harvest, that He would send forth labourers into His harvest.'—S. LUKE x. 2

THE thought of the harvest sets a very living parable before our minds. We shall not have a harvest if we do not sow anything in our fields. If we do not sow love, we shall not reap love : if we do not sow thoughts, we shall not reap ideas : if we do not sow faith, we shall not reap heaven.

Then the harvest brings us the thought of faith. The farmer has a heap of seed, and what is he going to do with it ? He is going to fling it away ! The text, ' Cast thy bread upon the waters,' is meant quite literally. People went out in boats and flung seed upon the waters of the Nile, and, as the water subsided, the seed sowed itself in the muddy ground. A good old priest once said, ' A great many men cast their bread upon the waters, but they tie a string to it first ! ' That is where we fail. We will not take a risk. Most of us need much more real faith in our religion.

Again, there is the thought of patience. The farmer has to wait a long time, and perhaps see his harvest destroyed. It is going on with patience that makes our character.

Then the day comes when the harvest is reaped. We do not want to limit the mercy of God, but our Lord does say that you cannot go on serving God and Mammon. There must come a harvest ; either of all your little failings, your little unstable ways, ultimately producing the harvest of a person who is not worth much ; or of all the little hidden acts of perseverance and faith and sacrifice, which will result in the harvest of a character which has a likeness to the character of Christ.

RECONCILIATION

THE whole Gospel of S. Luke is full of the spirit of reconciliation, the reconciliation of man with God, of person with person. The spirit of reconciliation is necessary in all ages. We may have perfect organization and perfect machinery, but, unless we have a right spirit behind them, they will not effect much. The forces of coercion on one side and revenge on the other will never do any good. Christ's religion reveals His spirit, and it is a reconciling spirit. Some people, wherever they go, bring trouble, and others bring blessing and healing, as did this great tender doctor, who was with S. Paul to the end, and must have had so sweet a character.

It is of the first importance that the world should be educated, and rightly educated. If a boy is taught to write beautifully, without a true teaching of morality, he may become a clever forger. If a man is taught the science of medicine without religious faith, he may become an inventor of poisonous drugs. One need not be afraid of education, but only of bad education : nor need we be afraid of the truth, but only of a half-truth. Our religion teaches us that the whole of life is one thing. The interest of India is the interest of England ; the interest of Germany is the interest of France ; the interest of men is the interest of women. We are one great family, and, as we are created in the image of our Father, it must be our joy, as it is our duty, to produce the perfect life of the true children of God, the life of men and women who can look into each other's eyes with courageous love, because they have the faith that can face any future without fear.

PERMANENCE, PROCESS, AND PROGRESS

'Being confident of this very thing, that He which began a good work in you will perfect it.'—PHIL. i. 6, R.V.

THERE is an element of permanence in life. Life itself is permanent. Things die, but life goes on. A rose grows and gives its beauty to the world, and then it withers and fades ; but the process that makes the rose is a permanent process, the life that was manifest in the rose is a permanent life. Personality is permanent. We pass on silently from youth to age, we have different bodies (our bodies change every ten years), but we are the same people. Truth is permanent. It is never really in danger. Truth abides in its majesty. Above all, God's love is permanent : the love of God abides for ever.

Life is also a process. It is not stagnant, it does not stop. If we cut a finger, immediately (unless there is something septic, which there ought not to be) the finger begins to heal. As we think of the processes of life, we see a third quality, progress. God's way is to make things develop progressively. There is the process and the progress by which a bulb becomes a lily. We see in all life the process and the progress.

Behind the permanence of our own personality, behind the process and the progress, is the eternal life of God, and He willed to reveal His eternal presence under the form of an incarnate life progressing from childhood to manhood, a life which was one life manifested through many things. We trust the great God, Who has begun in all His children the good work of life, by the processes of His wisdom to perfect that life, that it may become more and more worthy of His love, and at the last progress, through the refining power of the Holy Spirit, to the vision of His perfect beauty.

JUDGE NOT

'Her sins, which are many, are forgiven ; for she loved much.'
S. LUKE vii. 47

WHEN we are judging another we must remember that Someone is judging *us* : Jesus is looking right down into our heart, when we think we are looking down into some one else's. Simon the Pharisee thought he was looking into the woman's character and judging our Lord's prophetic insight : he had to learn that our Lord was looking into *his* character and judging his motives.

As we compare Simon and the woman, we see the difference between his hospitality and what we may call the hospitality of this poor sinful woman. Our Lord reveals Himself, as it were, as one seeking hospitality, and shows that He got a richer welcome from the poor woman, whom Simon judged, than He did from Simon, who presumed to judge not only the woman but Him, as not being a true prophet if He did not know who she was and whence she came. He showed that He knew both Simon and the woman. He judged these two souls, He judged their temptations, and He judged their approach to Himself, and He gave the pardon to the poor sinful woman, though He did not of course in any way minimize her sin. He said to her, ' Thy sins are forgiven. Go into peace.' That gives the full force of the Greek, and is a salutation full of depth and beauty—not just ' Go in peace,' but, ' Go into peace.'

We do not confess our sins to tell our Lord something that He does not know. He knew both Simon and the woman better than they knew themselves. We come that we may do our best to wash His feet with our penitence, to humble ourselves before we come to Him in Communion, as He humbled Himself so amazingly in His incarnate coming to us.

A DIVINE REVENGE

'God shall bring every work into judgement, with every secret thing, whether it be good, or whether it be evil.'—Eccles. xii. 14

It is a wonderful story that is told in 1 Samuel xxvi about Saul and David. There lay the king, who was seeking to kill David, in deep sleep under the stars, with his spear stuck in the ground beside him. David, from his experience as a shepherd, knew the way of the wilderness so well that he was able to penetrate the lines of the king's army, and stood with his companion looking down at his sleeping foe. How easy it would have been to give the strong son of Zeruiah permission to give one quick thrust of the spear and leave Saul there dead in the wilderness, and himself to have stepped into the kingdom, crowned by the outlaws who loved him ! Why could not David do it ? David, who often failed, did not fail then. He did the great splendid thing : he left the king unharmed, and took away the spear and the cruse of water, and knew that divine revenge which was surely taught him by the One Whose side was pierced with a spear in the days to come.

If we do something that is unworthy, we feel unhappy about it. It may be something that really does not hurt anybody, that does not hurt ourselves in any material way. Still it brings a shadow over our souls. Are we not sure that David, who had forgiven Saul, was a happy man that night and went back into the wilderness with a light heart, and that Saul went back to his palace ashamed ? Saul had sinned against 'the Father Who seeth in secret,' while David had done His will, that will which is always around us shaping the world to the kingdom of heaven.

THE LIFE OF COMMUNION

'Thy Father which seeth in secret.'—S. MATT. vi. 4

THE end of our religion is to bring about that sacred communion with the Father Who seeth in secret that our Lord knew. The Lord's Prayer was taught to the apostles after they had found our Lord in prayer. They had seen Him in communion with His Father, and that must have been an amazing and wonderful thing. They saw Him rapt in prayer, and when He came out of His prayer they said, 'Lord, teach us to pray.' He said, 'When ye pray, say, Our Father.'

The truly religious life is a life in which thoughts and words and actions all come out of our intercourse with the Father Who seeth in secret. So much of life may be just a game of tit for tat. A man does this because another man has done that, or to get something for nothing, or to get even with some one. Some one offends us and we answer back : some one flatters us and we fall in with their wishes. It is all very superficial, fugitive, and uncertain. But the person whose life is based upon prayer moves always quietly on to one end. Just as, when a great ship ploughs across the ocean, we see it move but do not see its motive power, because it is, as it were, hidden in its heart, so it is with the man who is living a spiritual life. His silences and his words, his actions and his abstinences, the whole movement of his life, are affected by a mysterious hidden power. He can never be bought or bribed, nor frightened out of the true way, because the whole motive of his life is communion with God. Our whole life should be this commerce and communion with the Father Who seeth in secret.

THE TRIUMPH OF SACRIFICE

'The prayers of all saints upon the golden altar which was before the throne.'—REV. viii. 3

WE are told in the Book of the Revelation that there is an altar in heaven, and that the saints find in it a meeting-place. It represents to them the supreme beauty, the vision of the perfect character of God, and it is also in their own experience the everlasting principle of their own redemption and sanctity. There is no one there who has arrived at his soul's home by any other way than this way of sacrifice. God's sacrifice has taught him to make his own ; God's plan has taught him to make his own, and the plan of his life is a pattern taught by God. The saint is not a person with a passionless obedience and no plan of his own : he is a person whose obedience is the passion of his own love's choice, and who has made deliberately the plan of his own life after the pattern of his adored Master's. There is not only a Sacrifice in heaven, but for redeemed humanity heaven is the result and creation of sacrifice.

We could not have known all that sacrifice means if we had never had the vision of the crucified Love on Calvary, and we could not have understood that, if we had not had our own capacity for pain and had that capacity put to the test. But out of that travail is born a love which, as it becomes more and more ready for sacrifice, becomes less and less troubled by pain, and will in the end rise through pain out of pain into that heaven which is the creation of the sacrifice of love.

FOURSQUARE

'The city lieth foursquare.'—Rev. xxi. 16

As in the Apocalypse the vision of the Church is unfolded to us as a city that ' lieth foursquare,' so we can say that the Church is four things.

It is a *home* wherein we find our loyalties ; wherein we find the spirit of the family, the relationships of the home ; wherein we gather round the common Table ; wherein we learn of our heredity, our ancestry, the saints of God ; wherein we are taught to make our own contribution to the good name of the family. *Noblesse oblige.* We must not lower the standard, we must not sully the fair name of the family of Christ.

It is a *hospital,* to which souls may come or may be brought, as was the palsied man to Christ in the Gospel story, and every priest should be ready at any time to perform the most delicate operation on a soul. It is a hospital where the surgeons can never be off duty, and where the remedies are really infallible, although the final healing may not be here.

It is a *school,* a school of sanctity, wherein the scholars are taught not so much to *do* as to *be,* to become saints ; wherein they are taught the apprehension of spiritual verities, and encouraged by the example of those who have attained to the highest degree of scholarship in sanctity. In a school of art people learn to see beauty, in a school of music to hear beauty, and in a school of science they learn to understand mysteries in the natural world. But in the school of sanctity the scholars are taught to *become* beautiful, in mind and affections and choice, and to apprehend mysteries in the spiritual sphere.

Lastly, before all and above all, the Church is *the Body of Christ.*

THE BODY OF CHRIST

'The glory of God did lighten it, and the Lamb is the light thereof.'
REV. xxi. 23

THE Church is the Body of Christ. When we come to Holy Communion, we have to remember it is not just *our* communion, but it is also *His* communion. It is not just that we want to bring 'our selves, our souls, our bodies,' to Him for His indwelling, but it is also that He wants to possess our humanity and make it the revelation of His own. Christ is surely still seeking a human nature wherein He may repeat the experiences of His incarnate life : feet that will follow the way of love, albeit they are pierced in the following ; hands that will succour and help and bless, although they may be wounded in their service ; a heart that will love, though the love be unrequited, and will bless though it be broken ; a will to choose the way of holiness and love and beauty, even though that way be the way of the Cross.

Even as the Sacred Humanity revealed the unseen God to such as had eyes to see, the Church in its highest sanctity does reveal the unseen Christ. Our Lord said, 'He that hath seen Me, hath seen the Father,' and He could say that because He could say, 'I and My Father are one.' He revealed the Father through His union with the Father, and when on the festivals of His saints we wonder at the self-sacrificing beauty of their lives, the explanation of it is their union with their Lord, and in them we see something of the beauty of Jesus. If the glory of God is revealed in the face of Christ, so the beauty of Christ is revealed in the calm faces of Christian saints.

SENSUALIST OR SAINT?

'They that are Christ's have crucified the flesh.'—GAL. v. 24

EITHER religion is a great delusion, or it is the one great reality. It is clear that either there is a world of spirit or there is not, and, if there is not, the only reality is the world of sense and appearance, and all talk of spiritual things would be untrue. Man would then be just a superior animal, with a physical equipment meant to react to physical things and no other. A person who lived quite consistently according to this theory, that sensation and appearance are the only realities, ought to be the happiest and most peaceful person; for surely it must produce greater happiness and peace to live according to a principle that is intrinsically true than to base your life on a theory which is radically false. But when men have lived according to this conception of reality, one can say quite certainly it has produced neither happiness nor beauty.

On the other hand, if we consider the generation of God's saints we see a company of people who have not lived in and responded to a merely physical world. These people have always existed in some sort since man has emerged from the mysterious background of the primeval past. There has always been the spiritual genius whom we call a saint, and his special characteristics have always been beauty of life and peace of soul. Judging from a purely critical point of view, it is surely a sounder theory to base your life upon that which produces beauty and peace than on principles that beget degradation and unrest. There is a better hope that we are on the road to reality if we keep in the Communion of the Saints than if we unite ourselves to the fellowship of the sensualists.

MIRACLES

'The wonderful works of God.'—ACTS ii. 11

OUR Lord's miracles can be divided into two classes. The miracles of providence, such as the stilling of the storm on the lake, represent a redemption of nature, a power of love coming into nature and making things that might have been a means of hurt become a means of blessing. They reveal a sovereign power. The miracles on man reveal a saving power, and so are greater, as the redemption of man is more glorious than the redemption of things. To our Lord sickness and death were the symptoms of a still deeper-lying malady, and the consummation of His miracles on man was in the raising of Lazarus, the last and clearest type of the Resurrection.

The miracles on man bring hope in signal distress. They reveal the possibilities of restoration and of the complete forgiveness of the spiritual evil from which in many cases the malady they healed had resulted. They are the outward and visible sign of the intercourse between life and the Author of life, and so they are sacramental. But they are not meant to be bulwarks of belief so much as treasures of faith and experience.

As Christ performed His miracles, they are signs of His coming kingdom. If He had simply wrought His miracles as God, they would have been portents ; if He, as man alone, had done them, they would have been prodigies. But in the miracles His perfect manhood acts in absolute harmony with His perfect divinity, often at the expense of an inward conflict of greatest agony. Each work of His was, like His last act, wrought at the expense of sacrifice. Each miracle is a microcosm of a world's redemption.

THE LAW OF CORRESPONDENCE

'Holiness, without which no man shall see the Lord.'—HEB. xii. 14

AT first sight these words from the Epistle to the Hebrews are rather terrifying. Yet after a moment or two of quiet thinking we see that the sentence is just one of life's axioms.

We can only see what the eyes that we bring to see will see. If we are colour-blind, though the fairest flower is put before us, its colour will mean nothing to us because we have no colour sense. We have eyes and ears, and, if those eyes and ears of ours are educated, we learn to see and hear beauty. Through the ages there have always been those whom we call artists, who were impelled to follow this quest, and have interpreted and contributed to this experience. Some have become eminent, and we speak of these as the 'Great Masters.'

If we are to 'see the Lord,' we must have a Christ-sense. There is something better than seeing or hearing beauty, and that is to become beautiful. Likeness to God is the condition of the Vision of God. When He was like to us in the Incarnation, He was only visible to those who were penitent and pure, that is, those who in a dim degree were getting to be like Him. Some have been specially eminent in their contribution to, and their interpretation of, this experience of spiritual beauty, and we call them 'Masters of the Spiritual Life.' Holiness enabled Isaiah to 'see the Lord,' though the vision could necessarily only be an interior vision ; while the lack of holiness prevented men from seeing the Lord when He walked this earth in exterior likeness to themselves.

SONG

'My songs will I make of Thy Name, O Thou Most Highest.'

Ps. ix. 2.

ALL great religions have expressed themselves in song, and there is no purer poetry than we find in the Psalms. Let us think what it is that makes people sing.

First of all, it is *love.* In the most English of all plays, *As You Like It*, we see Orlando going through the Forest of Arden with a radiant face, making songs of the name of Rosalind. The Blessed Francis, whose life was a melody and a poem, went singing through the world. There is something wrong with our religion if it ever drops wholly from a song to an argument. The soul that has realized the love of God must perforce go singing on its way.

The second thing that will teach the soul to sing will be *faith*, not only the love of the Divine Lover but faith in the Divine Lover. Every part of God's Church has known occasions of sorrow and sin. But the lovers of our Lord have always known that His love was greater than His Church's sin, and though they have seen most surely the sinfulness of the Church they have seen something more, the love of God, and in doing His will have found, as Jesus did, that the Cup of His will was also the chalice which gave them communion with His presence. So faith has taught the soulssaints to sing even in prison.

The third teacher of song is *hope.* The joy which was before our Lord when He accepted the Cross was His sure hope in the ultimate certain triumph of His Father's will. That hope may be ours also, and we can make our songs in the Name of the Most Highest better than David could, for we know that that sweet Name is the Name of Jesus.

NATURAL PRAYER

'He heareth the prayer of the righteous.'—Prov. xv. 29

WHEN we come to prayer, we want to put from us every selfish thought, everything that would give offence to the Sacred Presence of everlasting and perfect Love. When we have done our best to cleanse these souls of ours from all that is discordant with the purity and love of God, we must yield ourselves in silence to His holy inspiration, and quietly and naturally worship Him, and desire with all our power of desiring that His will may be done in us and all the world, and His kingdom of beauty and peace may come.

We may go into a place where a great many people are talking and doing things, and yet we know that nothing is really happening. Then we may go into a room where some one is suffering in silence, or into a church where a few people are kneeling in stillness, and this silence is pregnant with peace and power.

S. Anthony said some amazing words : ' No man is really praying who knows he is praying.' At first sight they seem absurd, but S. Anthony was one of the greatest experts in prayer the world has ever known. If we ponder what those words mean, the interpretation seems to be this. Just as, if a man is conscious of his breathing, he is not breathing quite normally ; or if a man is conscious that his heart is beating, it is not beating true ; so if we are conscious that we are praying, we have not attained to perfect prayer. Prayer at its highest is not self-expression but self-abandonment, and worship at its highest is not the making of sacrifices but the sacrifice of self. Such prayer is indeed conscious of God, but not conscious of itself.

HOPE AND FEAR

'The Lord will be the hope of His people.'—Joel iii. 16

' WHAT have we to expect ? Anything. What have we to hope for ? Everything. What have we to fear ? Nothing.' These words of Dr. Pusey are suitable for the occasion of the times we live in. We do well to make up our minds to *anything.* We in our generation ought not to desire that, having entered into the labours of those who have gone before us, we should escape from any travail pangs that may bring to birth the better things that we should be hoping for, for those who follow us. Dr. Pusey looked out on a Church in which the sense of the supernatural seemed extinct and spiritual experience practically unknown. Altars were receptacles for hats and umbrellas, and at S. Paul's Cathedral there were on Easter Day only six communicants, and yet he hoped for ' everything.' We have been allowed to see many things that he hoped for restored. But we have to look beyond the Church, not only to hope for a Church at unity in itself and one with the rest of Christendom, but for a world won for Christ, in which men have forgotten how to make war. The only thing we have to *fear* is our own instability. We have nothing to fear for God's cause. Truth will prevail, the kingdom will come, God's will be done, if not by us then by others.

In our case anything *may* happen. In our Lord's case He knew that the worst *would* happen. There is no doubt whatever as to what He expected (*S. Luke* xviii. 32, 33). To Him suffering was a certainty, but none the less He could say, ' I shall rise again.' He could hope for everything, as He feared nothing, because He knew He was in the way of the Divine Will.

FORGIVENESS

THE Gospel really means the goodness of God in forgiving our sins. Forgiveness is the great gift of God Himself to man. It does not mean any change in God, but the manifestation of God as He is. God created us that we might respond to His love, and when sin stopped this response *Love missed it*. Sin leaves man in a state of separation. God meets this state with an offer of forgiveness, restoration of the personal relationship. As man surrenders his will to God in penitence, he enters into the liberty of praise and service. The offer of forgiveness is conditioned by our forgivableness. Repentance is not just emotion : it is the return of the will to God.

The Divine forgiveness is based on the fact of the Incarnation. Our Lord accepted human nature as it was, and identifying Himself with humanity was 'made sin for us.' In His human nature He rendered that perfect obedience which atoned for sin, and His Sacrifice became efficacious for us, and so He became the sin-bearer of the world.

If a man has attained to the moral grandeur of winning in his own soul the power of completely forgiving another, and meeting his offence with love and the sincerity of a complete pardon, he brings to bear upon that other the strongest redeeming power there is in the world. The cost of forgiveness is borne really by the injured person. Completely to forgive another (which is a spiritual act that may take place quite alone) may be an act of great suffering. But only when a man has gone through this act can he really forgive. The Passion reveals what it cost God to forgive us.

POSITIVE PEACE

'A still more excellent way show I unto you.'—1 Cor. xii. 31, r.v.

It is the vocation of all who seriously claim Kingship for Christ our Lord in international as well as in ecclesiastical and personal affairs to realize that destructive methods will not have constructive results. There is a 'more excellent way' than the European way, which has been proved to be a failure, and that is the Christian way of forgiveness, which civilization has not yet tried.

Peace is a positive thing. It is not just abstaining from war : it must be the issue of that fellowship which should be bred of communion with the Prince of Peace, if there is any reality in that communion. To return good for evil is to rise above the human and to become saintly. To return the very highest good for the very worst evil is the revelation of the divine nature of Him Who in the same night He was betrayed treated us best when we treated Him worst, and gave us that Blessed Sacrament which is the soul and centre of our religion.

We must be very positively ' in love and charity with our neighbours,' and when we find ourselves asking the question of one of old time, ' Who is my neighbour ? ' we must listen afresh to the Master's story of ' The Good Samaritan,' and hear the teaching of His apostle, who would have us realize that in Christ there is ' neither bond nor free '—that is, class distinctions are swept aside ; ' neither Jew nor Greek '—that is, race prejudice is swept aside ; 'neither Barbarian nor Greek'—that is, we are to think internationally, not just nationally ; ' neither male nor female '—that is, even sex distinctions are transcended, and a true sex equality made possible. As the 'new man in Christ Jesus' appears, peace will appear with him in all its positive splendour.

OUR PEACE

'He is our peace.'—EPH. ii. 14

THE mind can only rest in truth, the moral sense in holiness, the imagination in beauty. When a thing attains to its end, it finds rest. As truth is the rest of the mind, and right is the rest of the moral sense, and beauty the goal of the imagination, so the Presence of God is the rest of the whole man. In union with the will of God only can we find our peace. Even as the sun at dawn shines out and brings to the world fulfilment, life, and happiness in the physical sphere, so there has shone out from the Incarnation and Passion of our Lord the light and the radiance of the Sun of Righteousness, which brings fulfilment, life, and peace in the spiritual sphere. How terrible would be a night without a dawn ! How futile life would be if the grave were really its ultimate and true end ! There is in S. John's Gospel a dramatic text : ' It was now dark, and Jesus had not yet come to them ' (vi. 17, R.V.). It tells of the spiritual night before the dawn of love breaks upon the troubled waters of life and brings peace.

There is peace in the vision of God. But the vision means vocation, and the price of peace is the reality of our obedience to our call. We need not be living some extraordinary life. He Himself chose the trade of a carpenter. Keeping your life clean and sweet, being a true comrade to others, you can make every day a following of Him. But as He followed the Father's will, we must follow in His footsteps, though it be through days of agony, knowing that if we are faithful they will bring us to Him Who is our peace.

THE VOCATION OF UNITY

'They have kept Thy word.'—S. JOHN xvii. 6

THE purpose of God is manifested in the unity of all He has made. We are called to unity as a vocation. As we seek unity with God, there will come a unity in our own being. But we shall only attain to unity with God as we *keep His word.* When He says, ' No,' we must not say, ' Yes.'

The challenges that come every hour of the day make for unity as we meet them in His spirit. God is always sounding a note, as it were, and we have to keep our conduct in tune with it, and make our lives a true harmony with the will and purpose of God. God's way is always the way of harmony, the way of fulfilling all that is best in us : it is never the way of suppression.

Our Lord ever sought the perfect unity of His will with the will of His Father, and so, though men slew Him, out of His death came that revelation of love and beauty which does act as a magnet to draw men of goodwill towards one another. Often there are things in others of which we cannot approve, but if we really are in unity with God our relationship with them will have redeeming value, whatever quality of pain there may be in some of the contacts that we must have with them. When things are wrong between other people and ourselves, the real secret of unity lies for us in our own souls. We must first get right with God ourselves. We cannot be in a wrong relationship with others if our wills are in union with the will of God.

THE UNITY OF THE CHURCH

'That they all may be one ; as Thou, Father, art in Me, and I in Thee, that they also may be one in us : that the world may believe that Thou hast sent Me.'—S. JOHN xvii. 21.

THE basic unity of the Church depends really on three great principles. The first is unity of vision. Those who see and love the same thing have a unity in that love which is a unity of freedom. They choose to follow the beauty that they see, and as they are all following the same splendour, they are united in their quest. So the unity that follows from the common love of the vision of our Lord is a very real unity.

Again, there is a unity that comes from an essential relationship of life. Those who are sacramentally united to Christ are essentially related to one another. Not only are they the children of the same Father, but by their communion they have claimed their relationship with Him. Their brotherhood is real. They have only got to realize it.

Thirdly, as people through the receiving of Christ attain to likeness with Him, there will come amongst them what may be called a family likeness. All who are like Him must be, to the degree in which they are like Him, like also to one another.

So following the same vision, receiving the same life, attaining to the same likeness, souls rise above the superficial distinctions of class or nation, and enter into that true unity which is the bond of the children of the kingdom of God. Our unity is in Him, our separations are in ourselves. As we attain to one-ness with Him, so we shall attain to union with one another in Him. This is really the Communion of Saints and that unity of the Church which has never been broken.

STRENGTH THROUGH COMMUNION

'I can do all things through Christ which strengtheneth me.'
PHIL. iv. 13

To man it is natural to have a limited life : to God it is natural to have an unlimited life. He does not keep that life to Himself ; He communicates it to His Son through the eternal forthgoing of God the Holy Spirit in the mystery of the Blessed Trinity.

The Son in the Incarnation took to Himself our human nature in order to reveal the eternal life of God. Our life is given us for the purpose of a growing acquaintance with God. It is not just existence, it does not consist in riches, it is not given us just that we may enjoy the beauty of the natural world. Life is *for* love, for communion with One Who *is* Love, for knowledge of a Personality Who is *all love*.

Not only has our Lord taken our human nature to interpret Love, but we ourselves have to rise to that love. We have to realize we are capable of great things. Many people go about as if they have been hypnotized, not realizing the powers that are hidden within them. Our Lord put Himself beside our littleness to give us not only the vision of Eternal Life, but the communication of that Life, that we might go along the way that He Himself went. The Eternal Life is revealed that we may follow it, not dream about it, but deliberately claim communion with it, and through that communion we shall have spiritual strength. Physical strength enables people to lift material weights. Spiritual strength enables them to bear sorrow, endure grief, love their enemies, and attain to spiritual valour.

WOUNDS, NOT WEAPONS

'The wrath of man worketh not the righteousness of God.'
S. Jas. i. 20

THE whole of our life is to be a testing and an education of our faith. The temptation always is to try to do God's work in our own faulty human fashion. We act as if we were afraid that God could not quite be trusted, and as if He perhaps needed our human diplomacy and human force to help Him. If, when people hit us, we yield to the inclination to hit back, by so doing we really deny the God and Father of our Lord Jesus Christ. The only war that is not both fatal and foolish is the war of the spirit, wherein we fight against the temptation to use human weapons instead of trusting the spiritual power of a fearless righteousness which has confidence that God our Father will completely vindicate Himself.

When our Lord came to this earth, He did not choose for Himself a desirable position and protect it by force, but He chose that which was so undesirable that no one else would dream of coveting it. He chose the poverty of Bethlehem and the pain of Calvary. Divine Love chose the lowest place, which only Divine Love could possibly have chosen.

As the wrath of man worketh not the righteousness of God, so also it will be true that the love of man, following in His footsteps, welcoming wounds and seeking to win through love and not through weapons, will work out the righteousness of God. Those principles of Divine Love which our Lord trusted, and which He proved to be true, we ourselves have to dare to trust too. We must do that very difficult thing—believe that the wounds of love are stronger than the weapons of men.

IN WHOSE IMAGE ?

'Whose is this image and superscription ? '—S. MATT. xxii. **20**

IF we take Adam as a type of the natural man, and ask in whose image he was created, we are told that it was in God's image. Man alone has mind, intelligence, reason, and a nature destined to be ennobled through the Incarnation. But the Divine Image has been defaced by sin.

If a portrait is spoilt, it can really only be restored by the artist who painted it. Human nature, the image of God, has been marred by sin, and the lost vision of humanity can only be restored by the Great Artist Himself. In the mystery of the Incarnation human nature has been re-drawn according to the perfect conception in the mind of God. That has been done once for all, and the beauty of that presentment can never be lost. Always before the gaze of God is that fair Image manifest and set against all caricatures and shameful distortions which have been produced by men.

The image and superscription upon a coin can no longer be seen if it is soiled. But when it has been cleaned both reappear. The soul smirched by sin may lose all sign of the Image in which it was made, but the cleansing of a real repentance will bring out again the true lineaments of a child of God.

When coins become defaced, they have to be re-minted. In the fire of the Sacred Passion the coin of human nature was re-minted, and the superscription of divine possession shone out upon it perfectly clearly. The agony of the passion of any life may be the re-minting of a coin for God's treasury.

WITH HIM

'He ordained twelve, that they should be with Him.'—S. MARK iii. 14

IF people who did not know their Bible very well were asked what was the text which told about the ordination of the apostles, they would probably say, ' He ordained twelve and gave them power,' or ' He ordained twelve and chose them to be the founders of His Church,' or ' He ordained twelve to preach the Gospel.' All these things would be true, but they would not give what we get in this verse, which gives us the root of the whole matter. This was the whole secret of the apostles' life. They *were* given power, and they *were* sent out to preach, and they *did* become the founders of the Church ; but all those things happened because of that first thing, that they knew a life of union with Jesus.

We must never let it go from us that our daily work is a very definite part of our religion. We can be with Jesus in our work. He was a working-man, and His days must often have been very tiresome and crowded days. We can imagine Him busy all day long, and yet that was glorifying God. The secret of our religion is not in the things that we say or do, but in the reasons and motives we have for saying or doing them. It is not just saying the Creed, which is so easy to do ; it is not making all sorts of professions, which is often not very hard to do ; but it is just to live with Jesus. If we can live a life of union with our Lord, there will issue from it something of that apostleship to which the twelve were called.

SPENDING

'There came a woman having an alabaster box of ointment of spikenard very precious ; and she brake the box, and poured it on His head.'—S. Mark xiv. 3.

Sometimes an act, which may not seem very important to some one who does not know the meaning of it, may mean a tremendous amount to the person who does it. To this poor woman the breaking of the alabaster cruse and the pouring of the rich ointment on our Saviour's head symbolized the giving of the whole treasure of her womanhood, the wonder of her life.

Our life is meant to be poured out, to be spent. All the great lives we have ever known have been poured out for others. When our Lord said those strange words about the harlots and publicans going into the kingdom of heaven before the Pharisees, His meaning appears to be that it is better to spend badly than not to spend at all. He seems to say : ' You Pharisees have hoarded your lives, so that no one has been the richer for them. These people have squandered their lives, their sins are many, but nevertheless they have spent them.' It may even be that it is better to spend money badly than to be a miser, to spend talent unwisely rather than not spend it at all. We *can*, and it is a very sad thing, spend our treasure badly, but we can learn by that spending.

Here is this woman, who has spent the treasure of her womanhood badly. Now she comes to Jesus, and in the light of His purity she sees the darkness and squalor of her life. But she pours out her treasure on His head, and in that act finds peace, and not only did she get blessing for herself but the whole house was filled with the odour of her spending. So the whole Church is enriched by every sacrificed and consecrated life.

THE HOPE BEFORE US

'Which hope we have as an anchor of the soul.'—HEB. vi. 19

WE cannot think of everything at once, so our Mother, the Church, very wisely says, ' Think of one particular thing. At Christmas think of the love of God, coming down to share the straw of poverty. In Lent think of the sorrow of God and your own sin. At Easter think of the triumph of God. At Ascensiontide think of spirituality. At Whitsuntide think of power. In Advent think of hope.'

Over the apparent hopelessness of our Lord's human circumstances there is always shining the star of a mystical hope. Could there have been anything more apparently hopeless than that of which we shall soon be thinking ? People might have said : ' A beggar's brat, born on a cold night, laid in a manger, cobwebs for his curtains, straw for his quilt.' Yet shining in the sky was the radiant star, around Him were the wondrous presences and the mystery beyond our life. What could have seemed more hopeless than a lonely half-dead man, stretched on the sand of the wilderness after forty days of fierce internal conflict ? Is *He* going to be the world's Saviour ? Yet angels ministered to Him. There again in the Garden, that sobbing man, with one friend stealing through the shadows to sell Him to the priests, His three most faithful overcome with sleep, the others quarrelling who shall be the greatest in the kingdom— is *He* going to be the Saviour of mankind ? Yet standing above Him is the angel of God. There are always those two notes about our Lord's revelation : the note of complete human simplicity, sympathy, and oneness with human nature ; and the note of divine overshadowing, the hope which is symbolized by the star and the angels, and the radiance that fell upon Him as He prayed on the Mount of Transfiguration.

176

BODY AND SOUL

'The hem of His garment.'—S. MATT. ix. 20

THIS poor woman in the Gospel story had a terrible cloud over her life. She was haunted by an incurable disease. She had in vain spent all her money on physicians in order to get that precious thing, sound health. Then she heard that Jesus was passing through her village, and drew near to Him in the crowd and touched Him with faith. She did not let it disquiet her or spoil her faith that so many seemed to be touching Him and not getting any good from Him. She said, ' If I may but touch His garment, I shall be whole.'

There are two basic principles at the bottom of all our sacramental faith, which are illustrated by this story : that the movement of the soul towards God meets with a movement of God towards the soul, and that all matter is really for the possession and expression of spirit. Here was this poor woman drawing near to Christ and receiving healing. She had contact with just the hem of His garment, and there came to her this healing, which made her material body healthy as well as bringing grace to her soul. God being so much greater, His movement towards the soul is a much more wonderful and complete movement. Here was the Divine Son of God, possessing this wondrous human body, which was for the possession and expression of His spirit.

It is spirit which gives to matter its real reason. It is the great spirit of God, the great presence of God behind the world, which gives the world its reason. The world would be just a sham thing if there were not behind it, indwelling it, informing it, directing it, the all-holy presence of the Creator God, the Triune Majesty.

THE SON OF MAN

'What is man ?'—Ps. viii. 4

WHAT is man ? Is he just an animal, doomed to die, with not even the caterpillar's hope of being a butterfly ? Or is this the real interpretation of all the pain and sorrow of life, that man is a spiritual being with a spiritual destiny ?

On a cold night there was a Baby born in a stable and laid on the straw, a little outcast, for Whom there was no room, even in an inn. We watch this Child fleeing to Egypt, because there was something strange about Him, and the king, hearing of it, tried to kill Him. He came back and worked in a shop. He talked to the people, and His teaching brought Him into conflict with the Church of His time. He was thrown over by everybody and ended on the gallows, a material destiny of absolute failure and catastrophe.

Yet He brings an answer to this great question, ' What is man ? ' and His answer is in the revelation of the spiritual destiny which He fulfilled. From the material point of view never was there such a failure and tragedy : from the spiritual point of view there never was, and never can be, so great a splendour as that spiritual destiny which the Resurrection and Ascension have revealed.

Man is God's child. He has a spiritual home waiting for him, a spiritual language to learn, a spiritual Food on which to nourish himself. Man's end is rest with God and co-operation with God in all the purposes of the divine will. In difficulty and darkness his character is being shaped, his soul is being enriched and formed, learning to know its true destiny, the destiny of a son of God.

IN A DESERT PLACE

'Come ye yourselves apart into a desert place, and rest awhile.'
S. Mark vi. 31

The Jews have a saying, ' All good things come from the wilderness. Thence came the Law and the Manna and the Ark.' The great souls of all time have sought solitude, and God has made Himself known to them. ' If ye seek Him, ye shall surely find Him,' said one of them, and the best of them proved that to be true in their own personal experience.

Every one ought to get away every year, and to get out every day. In the same way, we ought to have a retreat every year, and a bit of a retreat, if only for a few minutes, every day. Each one of us should have his recognized oratory. It may be known only to himself. It may be a walk in a wood, or a corner of a church or of a room. People sometimes pray in a particular street on their way home from work, or nurses going up a special staircase in a hospital. But we ought to have our covenanted time and place. Our Lord's oratory was sometimes a garden, and perhaps a cave in the garden when He wanted to be still more deeply hidden.

The real movement in the world is a spiritual movement, a movement of prayer. If we change ourselves, our environment will change itself. If we change ourselves, the world will change itself. Our Lord always had confidence in the unseen. If we are true to His most vital teaching, we shall believe that in solitude we may have our closest communion with the presence of God, and in silence may hear most clearly the message of His will. As the soul passes to union with God, so the whole life takes to itself more and more the quality of prayer.

PEACE IN A PRISON

*'The peace of God, which passeth all understanding, shall keep your
hearts and minds through Christ Jesus.'*—PHIL. iv. 7

It is a wonderful thought that the words which give us
our great liturgical blessing were written in a prison. How
was it that Paul the apostle was able in his chains to write about
peace ? It was because his soul had attained to such complete
union with his Lord that things of time and sense and
material moment had ceased to have any effect upon him.
He saw all things now from the supernatural point of view
and spiritual values were the only currency which counted
with him. 'The Lord,' he says, ' is at hand. . . . Rejoice
in the Lord alway : and again I say, rejoice.'

These words of blessing were probably written only two
years before his martyrdom. He had very nearly finished
his course, and he knew that he had fought a good fight. The
deep peace that his self-oblation had brought to him enabled
him to turn the experience of his own soul into these beautiful
words of valediction, and so bequeath to the Church for all
time the great blessing which ends its greatest act of worship.

We are told on another occasion of a light shining in a
prison. We have the vision here of peace in the soul of a
prisoner. Just before His Passion our Lord spoke most of
peace. It is fitting that His great apostle should have
followed Him in this, that when he was so near to death at
the hands of Nero he should have been able to write, as he did
in this last chapter of his letter to the Philippians, words
which tell of a heart overflowing with love, of a spirit
soaring in liberty, and a soul altogether at peace.

INDEX OF BIBLICAL REFERENCES